Invasive Exotic Plant Monitoring at Hopewell Culture National Historical Park

Year 2 (2011)

Natural Resource Technical Report NPS/HTLN/NRDS—2012/346

Craig C. Young, Jordan C. Bell, Chad S. Gross, and Ashley D. Dunkle

National Park Service, Heartland I&M Network
Wilson's Creek National Battlefield
6424 West Farm Road 182
Republic, MO 64738

Heartland Network

Natural Resource Monitoring

July 2012

U.S. Department of the Interior
National Park Service
Natural Resource Stewardship and Science
Fort Collins, Colorado

The National Park Service, Natural Resource Stewardship and Science office in Fort Collins, Colorado publishes a range of reports that address natural resource topics of interest and applicability to a broad audience in the National Park Service and others in natural resource management, including scientists, conservation and environmental constituencies, and the public.

The Natural Resource Data Series is intended for the timely release of basic data sets and data summaries. Care has been taken to assure accuracy of raw data values, but a thorough analysis and interpretation of the data has not been completed. Consequently, the initial analyses of data in this report are provisional and subject to change.

All manuscripts in the series receive the appropriate level of peer review to ensure that the information is scientifically credible, technically accurate, appropriately written for the intended audience, and designed and published in a professional manner.

This report received informal peer review by subject-matter experts who were not directly involved in the collection, analysis, or reporting of the data. Data in this report were collected and analyzed using methods based on established, peer-reviewed protocols and were analyzed and interpreted within the guidelines of the protocols.

This report is available from the Heartland I&M Network website (http://www.nature.nps.gov/im/units/htln/) on the internet and the Natural Resource Publications Management website (http://www.nature.nps.gov/publications/nrpm/).

Please cite this publication as:

NPS 353/116003, July 2012

Contents

Figures

Figures (continued)

Figures (continued)

Figures (continued)

Tables

Introduction

A review of NPS species, the national database registering plant occurrence in parks, indicated that 465 plant species occurred in Hopewell Culture National Historical Park. Of these, 148 (32%) are non-native, meaning that these plants were recently introduced through human agency. Furthermore, 39% of these non-native species were classified as common. Based on a screening that attempts to identify plants as not only non-native, but also invasive (Young et al. 2007), 47 (32%) of the non-native plants were also noted as invasive. Invasive plants spread rapidly once established and are the plants most likely to pose problems for land managers. While no federal noxious weeds are known from the park, six state noxious weeds are present: Canada thistle (*Cirsium arvense*), Johnsongrass (*Sorghum halepense*), nodding plumeless thistle (*Carduus nutans*), poison hemlock (*Conium maculatum*), Queen Anne's lace (*Daucus carota*), and wild parsnip (*Pastinaca sativa*). Also, 16 of the 26 species identified on the Ohio Invasive Plants Council list occur in the park. Clearly, invasive plants are a resource management issue for the park.

Methods

Watch lists

Invasive exotic plant species on two watch lists were sought during monitoring (Table 1). Plants designated as high priority invasive species (Young et al. 2007) and not known to occur on the park per IRMA, NPSpecies Application (https://irma.nps.gov/App/Portal/Home) constituted the "early detection watch list". Designated invasive exotic plants known to occur on the park per NPSpecies constitute the "park-established watch list". Black locust (*Robinia pseudocacaia*) was also included on the park established list, but is native to the United States, Ohio, and possibly the area near Hopewell Culture National Historical Park, but is often invasive. While aquatic species are listed on the watch lists, terrestrial plants were the focus of this survey.

Field methods

Invasive exotic plant species on designated watch lists (Table 1) were sought in high priority areas in Hopewell Culture National Historical Park (Figure 1). These high priority areas consisted of areas with woods or restored prairies and measured 223.2 acres in area. Kristen Bates with Davey Resource Group conducted the first survey from June 17-18 and August 4-8, 2008. Dr. Steven Brewer with Copperhead Consulting and Ms. Kyla Hershey with Lawhon and Associates, Inc. used a Garmin 60CSx and Trimble Instruments model GeoXT handheld GPS units to conduct the second survey during July 7-16, 2011. Surveys were conducted in search units approximately 2 acres in size. Three equidistant passes through each search unit were made, though entire polygons were not fully searched. Observers recorded line transects to identify invasive exotic plants in an approximately 3- to 12-m belt. The widest belt possible was used, but varied depending on site conditions. Belt widths likely also varied to some degree among observers. Coarse cover values (0=0, 1=0.1-0.9 m^2, 2=1-9.9 m^2, 3=10-49.9 m^2, 4= 50-99.9 m^2, 5=100-499.9 m^2, 6= 500-999.9 m^2, 7= 1,000-4,999 m^2) were attributed to each species per search unit. A total of 321 transects within 107 search units were searched.

Analytical methods

The estimates of plant cover for each invasive species on the park required calculation of the fraction of the area searched during the survey. Calculations of the observed reference frame fraction were made by multiplying transect length, the number of transects, and the belt width. The belt width was either 3 m (the minimum possible width) or 12 m (the maximum possible width). Transect length was calculated by summing the lengths of the 321 transects. The product was then divided by the reference frame area (Eq. 1).

Eq.1. Fraction of area searched = *transect length * number of transects * belt width*
reference frame area

The minimum fraction of area searched (belt width = 3 m) was 10%, and the maximum fraction of area searched (belt width = 12 m) was 40%.

To calculate the minimum end of the estimated cover range for each species, the lower endpoints associated with the assigned cover class values for that species were summed and then divided by the reference frame fraction observed assuming the widest possible survey belt (i.e., maximum fraction observed) (Eq. 2).

Eq.2. Minimum cover estimate = *Σ low end of cover value range for species*
fraction of area searched assuming 12-m belt width

Maximum cover for each species was calculated similarly, using the upper endpoints of the cover values in each occupied search unit and assuming that a 3 m belt was surveyed (i.e., minimum fraction of area observed) (Eq. 3).

Eq. 3. Maximum cover estimate = *Σ high end of cover value range for species*
fraction of area searched assuming 3-m belt width

Taken together, the minimum and maximum cover estimates provide an estimated range of cover that accounts for the uncertainty arising from the sampling method. Non-overlapping ranges represent the strongest evidence for differences in abundance.

The park-wide frequency of invasive exotic plants was calculated as the percentage of occupied search units (Eq. 4).

Eq. 4. Frequency of an invasive plant species = *Σ units occupied by species* *100*
Σ units sampled

The invasive exotic plants encountered at Hopewell Culture National Historical Park were attributed to line transects in a GIS and mapped (Figures 3-48).

Invasiveness ranks

To provide additional information on the ecological impact and feasibility of control, the ecological impact and general management difficulty sub-ranks that constitute the invasiveness rank (I-rank), as determined by NatureServe (Morse et al. 2004), were listed when available. The ecological impact characterized the effect of the plant on ecosystem processes, community composition and structure, native plant and animal populations, and the conservation significance of threatened biodiversity. General management difficulty ranks were assigned based on the resources and time generally required to control a plant, the non-target effects of control on native populations, and the accessibility of invaded sites. Sub-ranks were given as high (H), medium (M), low (L), insignificant (I), unknown (U), or a combination of ranks.

Results and Discussion

In 2008 and 2011, a cumulative total of 46 of the 105 (44%) taxa present on both watch lists were documented in Hopewell Culture National Historic Park. Of these, 12 of 65 (18%) species from the early detection list and 34 of 40 (85%) species from the park established list were found. Twelve species not recorded in 2008 were observed in the 2011 survey, while the converse was true for four species.

Invasive Plant Frequency

Invasive plant species were widespread in Hopewell Culture National Historical Park. Of the 30 species found during both surveys, 12 species (40%) occupied at least 25% of search units in 2011, while only 7 (23%) occupied less than 5% of search units. Overall, the frequency increased for 66.6% and decreased for 33.3% of species from 2008 to 2011. Of the 16 species found during only a single survey, 11 (69%) occupied less than 5% of search units in 2011. The species that did not follow this pattern likely reflected problems related to field identification and target list construction. Tall fescue was likely overlooked during 2008 as the species was found in 62% of transects in 2011. The identification of two bush honeysuckle species was apparently mixed-up as the frequency of Morrow's honeysuckle (*Lonicera morrowii*) and Tatarian honeysuckle (*L. tatarica*) were very similar, but each was found only during alternate years. This issue will be resolved during subsequent surveys. Perennial rye (*Lolium perenne*) may have been overlooked in 2008 as the plant was found in over 12% of search units in 2011. Bald brome (*Bromus racemosus*), on the other hand, was not sought at all in 2008, which accounts for its absence that year.

Invasive Plant Abundance

Between 2008 and 2011, abundance increased for the great majority of species found in Hopewell Culture National Historical Park (Table 2). The consistency in the direction and magnitude of these increases suggested strong observer differences between years rather than actual increases. In spite of this observer error, the abundance ranks remained somewhat ordered with eight of the ten most abundant species in 2008 also being among the ten most abundant in 2011. Amur honeysuckle (*Lonicera maackii*), with the highest potential cover in 2011, covered at least 0.4 acres in 2008 and at least 7.0 acres in 2011. In 2011, maximum potential cover of 11 of 46 invasive exotic plants exceeded 10 acres. This included five herbaceous species (Canada thistle [*Cirsium arvense*], common periwinkle [*Vinca minor*], garlic mustard [*Alliaria petiolata*], ground ivy [*Glechoma hederacea*], and Japanese honeysuckle [*Lonicera japonica*]), two bush (amur and Tatarian) honeysuckle species, two tree species (autumn olive [*Elaeagnus umbellata*] and black locust [*Robinia pseudoacacia*]), a cool season grass (tall fescue, [*Schedonorus phoenix*]), and a shrub (multiflora rose [*Rosa multiflora*]). This assemblage of invasive plant species reflects the potential for impact in most portions of the park. Fortunately, 30 of the 46 invasive species recorded in 2011 occupied at most less than 2 acres. Based on the sum of the minimum cover estimates for all species encountered in each survey, total invasive plant cover in the park increased from at least 2.9 acres in 2008 to at least 31.8 acres in 2011. This represented 1.3% and 14.2%, respectively, of the 223.2 acre study area. Amur honeysuckle, Japanese honeysuckle, and tall fescue accounted for the majority of this difference.

Changes in Invasive Plant Abundances

Despite observer differences, non-overlapping abundance estimates continue to provide the strongest indicator of change in abundance between time periods. Based on non-overlapping cover ranges, we identified four species as increasing from the 2008 survey: amur honeysuckle, Canada thistle, common periwinkle, and Johnsongrass . These increases similarly matched increases in frequency. Although cover ranges overlaped, autumn olive and black locust also demonstrated considerable increases in cover between survey periods. We interpreted the rest of the overlapping ranges as reflecting general similarity in abundance between 2008 and 2011.

Implications for Invasive Plant Management

Invasive plant management scenarios (Figure 1) may assist the parks in strengthening rationale and priorities for invasive plant management. In our opinion, the forests in which this study was conducted represented areas with the highest natural resource value in the park. Because the park's mandate per its enabling legislation focuses on cultural resource protection, the role of these forests in the cultural landscape is unclear as the park does not have a cultural landscape report. Our opinion is that invasive plant control projects at HOCU will likely fall under the scenarios characterized as precautionary actions or as a scenario requiring cost-benefit analysis. While it is difficult to identify clear boundaries between these projects, we suggest that a maximum abundance of 0.5 acres may serve as a reasonable dividing line. In this case, 21 of 46 species would be considered to be plants with relatively low abundance that should be eradicated as a precaution. Decisions regarding the remaining 25 species could benefit from additional considerations of the potential costs and benefits. These decisions, however, are the purview of the park and are not analyzed here. Finally, legal requirements such as noxious weed laws may require that the park manage certain invasive plant species.

Literature Cited

Morse, L. E., J. M. Randall, N. Benton, R. D. Hiebert, and S. Lu. 2004. An Invasive Species Assessment Protocol: Evaluating Non-Native Plants for Their Impact on Biodiversity. Version 1. Document. Online. <http://www.natureserve.org/getData/plantData.jsp#InvasivesProtocol>. Accessed 1 December 2006.

NPSpecies - The National Park Service Biodiversity Database. IRMA version. https://irma.nps.gov/Species.mvc/Welcome (accessed 16 February 2012).

Young, C.C., J.L. Haack, L.W. Morrison, and M.D. DeBacker. 2007. Invasive exotic plant monitoring protocol for the Heartland Inventory and Monitoring Program. Natural Resource Report NPS/HTLN/NRR-2007/018. National Park Service, Fort Collins, Colorado.

Hopewell Culture National Historic Park
Exotic Plant Search Units

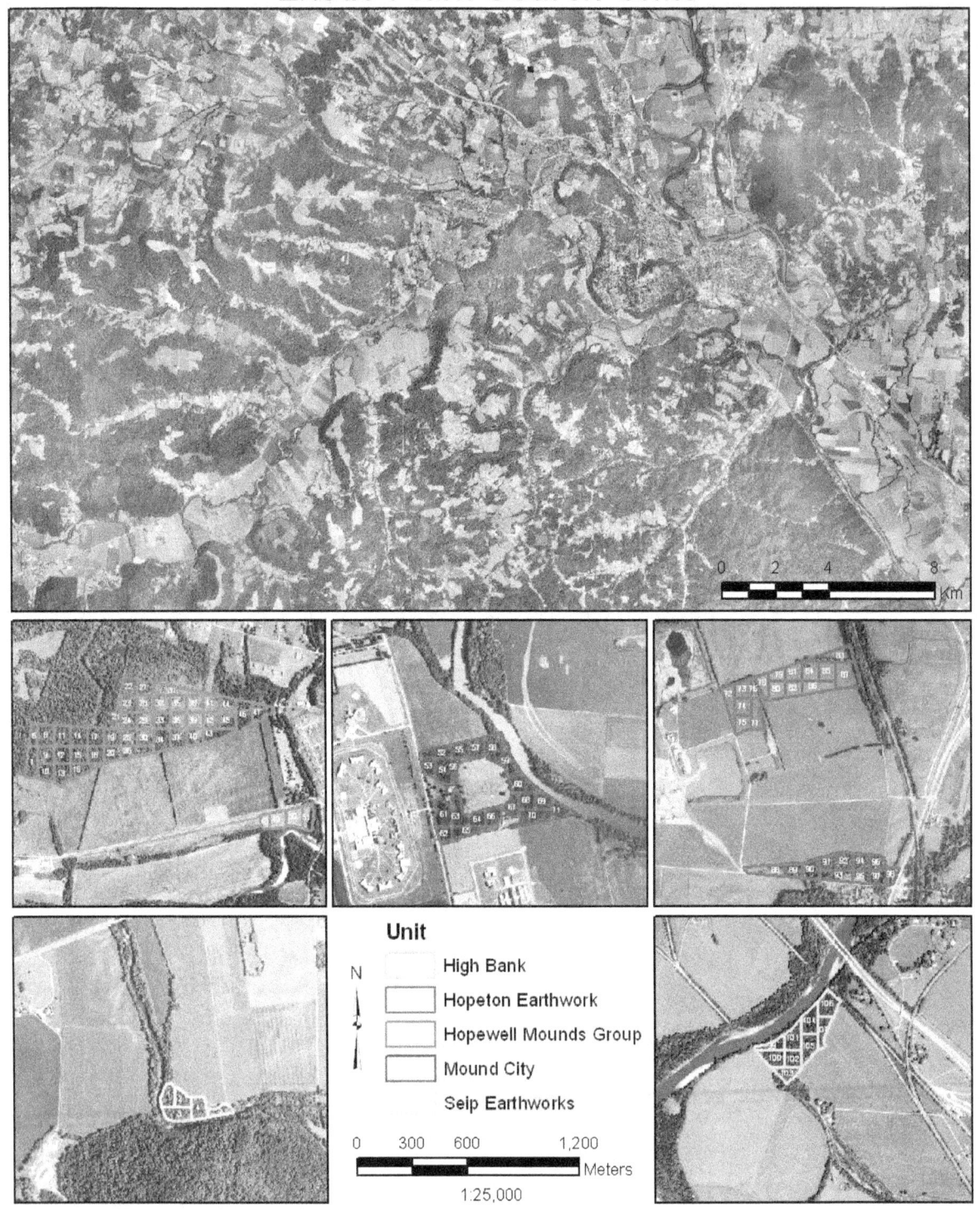

Figure 1. Invasive plant search units (n=107) on Hopewell Culture National Historical Park. Search units focused on restored prairies and intact forests on the park.

Table 1. Watch lists for Hopewell Culture National Historical Park.

Early Detection Watch List		Park-Established Watch List	
Amur maple	*Acer ginnala*	Tree of heaven	*Ailanthus altissima*
Norway maple	*Acer platanoides*	Silktree	*Albizia julibrissin*
European alder	*Alnus glutinosa*	Garlic mustard	*Alliaria petiolata*
Amur peppervine	*Ampelopsis brevipedunculata*	Lesser burdock	*Arctium minus*
Bald brome	*Bromus racemosus*	Japanese barberry	*Berberis thunbergii*
Poverty brome	*Bromus sterilis*	Smooth Brome	*Bromus inermis*
Flowering rush	*Butomus umbellatus*	Cheatgrass	*Bromus tectorum*
Oriental bittersweet	*Celastrus orbiculatus*	Nodding plumeless thistle	*Carduus nutans*
Yellow star-thistle	*Centaurea solstitialis*	Canada thistle	*Cirsium arvense*
Spotted knapweed	*Centaurea stoebe ssp. micranthos*	Bull thistle	*Cirsium vulgare*
Crownvetch	*Coronilla varia*	Queen Anne's lace	*Daucus carota*
Louise's swallow-wort	*Cynanchum louiseae*	Fuller's teasel	*Dipsacus fullonum*
Chinese yam	*Dioscorea oppositifolia*	Russian olive	*Elaeagnus angustifolia*
Cutleaf teasel	*Dipsacus laciniatus*	Ground ivy	*Glechoma hederacea*
Brazilian waterweed	*Egeria densa*	Orange daylily	*Hemerocallis fulva*
Autumn olive	*Elaeagnus umbellata*	Dames rocket	*Hesperis matronalis*
Russian olive	*Elaeagnus umbellate/ angustifolia*	Common St. Johnswort	*Hypericum perforatum*
Quackgrass	*Elymus repens*	Common motherwort	*Leonurus cardiac*
Burningbush	*Euonymus alata*	European privet	*Ligustrum vulgare*
Winter creeper	*Euonymus fortunei*	Japanese honeysuckle	*Lonicera japonica*
Cypress spurge	*Euphorbia cyparissias*	Amur honeysuckle	*Lonicera maackii*
Leafy spurge	*Euphorbia esula*	Tatarian honeysuckle	*Lonicera tatarica*
Glossy buckthorn	*Frangula alnus*	Creeping jenny	*Lysimachia nummularia*
English ivy	*Hedera helix*	Sweetclover	*Melilotus officinalis*
Common velvetgrass	*Holcus lanatus*	White mulberry	*Morus alba*
Japanese hop	*Humulus japonicus*	Wild parsnip	*Pastinaca sativa*
Paleyellow iris	*Iris pseudacorus*	Princesstree	*Paulownia tomentosa*
Shrub lespedeza	*Lespedeza bicolor*	Kentucky bluegrass	*Poa pratensis*
Sericea lespedeza	*Lespedeza cuneata*	Sulphur cinquefoil	*Potentilla recta*
Border privet	*Ligustrum obtusifolium*	Mahaleb cherry	*Prunus mahaleb*
Butter and eggs	*Linaria vulgaris*	Black locust	*Robinia pseudoacacia*
Tall fescue	*Lolium arundinaceum*	Multiflora rose	*Rosa multiflora*
Meadow fescue	*Lolium pratense*	Common sheep sorrel	*Rumex acetosella*
Ryegrass	*Lolium spp*	Rumex crispus	*Rumex crispus*
Morrow's honeysuckle	*Lonicera morrowii*	Bouncingbet	*Saponaria officinalis*
Showy fly honeysuckle	*Lonicera X bella*	Johnsongrass	*Sorghum halepense*
Bird's-foot trefoil	*Lotus corniculatus*	Spreading hedgeparsley	*Torilis arvensis*
Narrow-leaf bird's-food trefoil	*Lotus tenuis*	Siberian elm	*Ulmus pumila*
Purple loosestrife	*Lythrum salicaria*	Common mullein	*Verbascum thapsus*
Nepalese browntop	*Microstegium vimineum*	Common periwinkle	*Vinca minor*
Chinese silvergrass	*Miscanthus sinensis*		

Table 1. (continued)

Early Detection Watch List		Park-Established Watch List
Myosotis scorpioides	True forget-me-not	
Myriophyllum aquaticum	Parrot feather watermilfoil	
Myriophyllum spicatum	Eurasian watermilfoil	
Najas minor	Brittle waternymph	
Onopordum acanthium	Scotch cottonthistle	
Phalaris arundinacea	Reed canarygrass	
Phragmites australis	Common reed	
Poa compressa	Canada bluegrass	
Polygonum cuspidatum	Japanese knotweed	
Polygonum perfoliatum	Asiatic tearthumb	
Polygonum sachalinense	Giant knotweed	
Populus alba	White poplar	
Potamogeton crispus	Curly pondweed	
Pueraria montana var. lobata	Kudzu	
Pyrus calleryana	Callery pear	
Rhamnus cathartica	Common buckthorn	
Rorippa nasturtium-aquaticum		
Sonchus arvensis	Field sowthistle	
Spiraea japonica	Japanese meadowsweet	
Tanacetum vulgare	Common tansy	
Torilis japonica	Erect hedgeparsley	
Typha angustifolia	Narrowleaf cattail	
Typha X glauca		
Viburnum opulus	European cranberrybush	
Wisteria floribunda	Japanese wisteria	

8

Table 2. Overview of invasive exotic plants found in Hopewell Culture National Historical Park. Ecological impact and general management difficulty based on NatureServe I-Rank subranks (Morse et al. 2004). Subranks are given as high (H), medium (M), low (L), insignificant (I), unknown (U), a range of ranks (indicated by *I*), or not available (--).

Scientific Name	Common Name	Watch list	2008 Park-wide cover (acres)	2011 Park-wide cover (acres)	2008 Frequency (%)	2011 Frequency (%) (Difference 2008-2011)	Ecological impact	Management difficulty
Lonicera maackii	Amur honeysuckle	Park Established	0.4 – 5.9	7.0-117.0	63.6	76.6(13)	HM	M
Lonicera japonica	Japanese honeysuckle	Park Established	0.7 – 10.2	6.1-101.2	59.8	78.5 (18.7)	M	HM
Schedonorus phoenix	Tall fescue	Early Detection	0	4.2-77.0	0	61.7(61.7)	M	HM
Elaeagnus umbellata	Autumn olive	Early Detection	0.2 – 3.0	2.1-42.5	30.8	28.0(-2.8)	H	L
Vinca minor	Common periwinkle	Park Established	0.05 – 0.7	2.0-38.5	6.5	10.3(3.8)	I	U
Glechoma hederacea	Ground ivy	Park Established	0.3 – 4.8	2.0-32.5	32.7	43.0(10.3)	MI	U
Rosa multiflora	Multiflora rose	Park Established	0.4 – 4.8	1.8-29.1	60.7	67.3(6.6)	L	L
Alliaria petiolata	Garlic mustard	Park Established	0.5 – 8.8	1.0-14.5	53.3	69.2(15.9)	ML	M
Cirsium arvense	Canada thistle	Park Established	0.04 – 0.9	1.0-14.4	19.6	23.4(3.8)	ML	HM
Robinia pseudoacacia	Black locust	Park Established	0.1 – 2.1	0.9-12.0	23.4	30.8(7.4)	HM	M
Lonicera morrowii	Morrow's Honeysuckle	Early Detection	0	0.9-12.9	0	21.5(21.5)	ML	M
Sorghum halepense	Johnsongrass	Park Established	0.006 – 0.3	0.5-8.7	12.1	20.6(8.5)	ML	HM
Lysimachia nummularia	Creeping jenny	Park Established	0.01 – 0.6	0.4-6.6	21.5	34.6(13.1)	L	L
Morus alba	White mulberry	Park Established	0.04 – 0.9	0.4-6.6	15.9	16.8(0.9)	ML	ML
Bromus tectorum	Cheatgrass	Park Established	0.03 – 0.8	0.5-6.1	18.7	20.6(1.9)	H	HM
Daucus carota	Queen Anne's lace	Park Established	0.04 – 1.2	0.3-5.5	44.9	50.5(5.6)	I	I
Lolium perenne	Perennial ryegrass	Early Detection	0	0.1-2.0	0	12.1(12.1)	M	MI
Poa (pratensis)	Kentucky bluegrass	Park Established	0.02 – 0.6	0.08-1.9	24.3	26.2(1.9)	M	ML
Bromus inermis	Smooth brome	Park Established	0.02 – 0.5	0.09-1.9	12.1	7.5(-4.6)	M	ML

9

Table 2. (continued)

Scientific Name	Common Name	Watch list	2008 Park-wide cover (acres)	2011 Park-wide cover (acres)	2008 Frequency (%)	2011 Frequency (%) (Difference 2006-2011)	Ecological impact	Management difficulty
Bromus racemosus	Bald brome	Park Based	Not sought	0.09-1.1	0	15(15)	MI	U
Ligustrum vulgare	European privet	Park Established	0.004 – 0.2	0.05-1.1	8.4	19.6(11.2)	HL	HM
Rumex crispus	Curly dock	Park Established	0.006 – 0.2	0.03-1.0	18.7	29.0(10.3)	HM	M
Torilis arvensis	Spreading hedgeparsley	Park Established	0.01 – 0.5	0.04-1.0	18.7	19.6(0.9)	----	----
Lonicera tatarica	Tatarian honeysuckle	Park Established	0.03 – 0.8	0	25.2	0(-25.2)	M	M
Potentilla recta	Sulphur cinquefoil	Park Established	0.002 – 0.09	0.002-0.8	9.3	3.7(-5.6)	HL	ML
Melilotus officinalis	Sweetclover	Park Established	0.008 – 0.3	0.02-0.5	16.8	12.1(-4.7)	M	M
Berberis thunbergii	Japanese barberry	Park Established	0.003 – 0.1	0.02-0.5	4.7	8.4(3.7)	HM	I
Pastinaca sativa	Wild parsnip	Park Established	0.002 – 0.09	0.04-0.5	10.3	8.4(-1.9)	LI	L
Ailanthus altissima	Tree-of-heaven	Park Established	0	0.02-0.4	0	3.7(3.7)	ML	ML
Microstegium vimineum	Nepalese browntop	Early Detection	0	0.04-0.4	0	1.9(1.9)	M	HM
Saponaria officinalis	Bouncingbet	Park Established	0	0.01-0.3	0	3.7(3.7)	I	U
Euonymus alata	Burningbush	Early Detection	0.003 – 0.1	0.007-0.2	7.5	2.8(-4.7)	LI	L
Phalaris arundinacea	Reed canarygrass	Early Detection	0.003 – 0.1	0.008-0.2	5.6	3.7(-1.9)	H	HM
Dipsacus fullonum	Fuller's teasel	Park Established	0.002 – 0.08	0.007-0.2	3.7	2.8(-0.9)	L	ML
Arctium minus	Lesser burdock	Park Established	0.001 – 0.03	0.004-0.1	1.9	6.5(4.6)	LI	MI
Celastrus orbiculatus	Oriental bittersweet	Early Detection	0	0.007-0.1	0	1.9(1.9)	ML	M
Polygonum cuspidatum	Japanese knotweed	Early Detection	0	0.006-0.1	0	0.9(0.9)	HM	M
Pyrus calleryana	Callery pear	Early Detection	0	0.006-0.1	0	0.9(0.9)	LI	ML
Verbascum thapsus	Common mullein	Park Established	0.0001 – 0.004	0.002-0.1	1.9	3.7(1.8)	ML	L

Table 2. (continued)

Scientific Name	Common Name	Watch list	2008 Park-wide cover (acres)	2011 Park-wide cover (acres)	2008 Frequency (%)	2011 Frequency (%) (Difference 2006-2011)	Ecological impact	Management difficulty
Cirsium vulgare	Bull thistle	Park Established	0.001 – 0.03	0.001-0.05	3.7	2.8(-0.9)	ML	ML
Bromus sterilis	Poverty brome	Early Detection	0	0.001-0.02	0	0.9(0.9)	ML	U
Hemerocalis fulva	Orange daylily	Park Established	0.004 – 0.1	0.001-0.02	5.6	0.9(-4.7)	MI	L
Ulmus pumila	Siberian elm	Park Established	0	0.0001-0.002	0	0.9(0.9)	ML	ML
Hesperis matronalis	Dame's rocket	Park Established	0.003 – 0.1	0	4.7	0(-4.7)	MI	HL
Leonurus cardiaca	Common motherwort	Park Established	0.0001 – 0.002	0	0.9	0(-0.9)	----	----
Prunus mahaleb	Mahaleb cherry	Park Established	0.001 – 0.02	0	0.9	0(-0.9)	LI	U

11

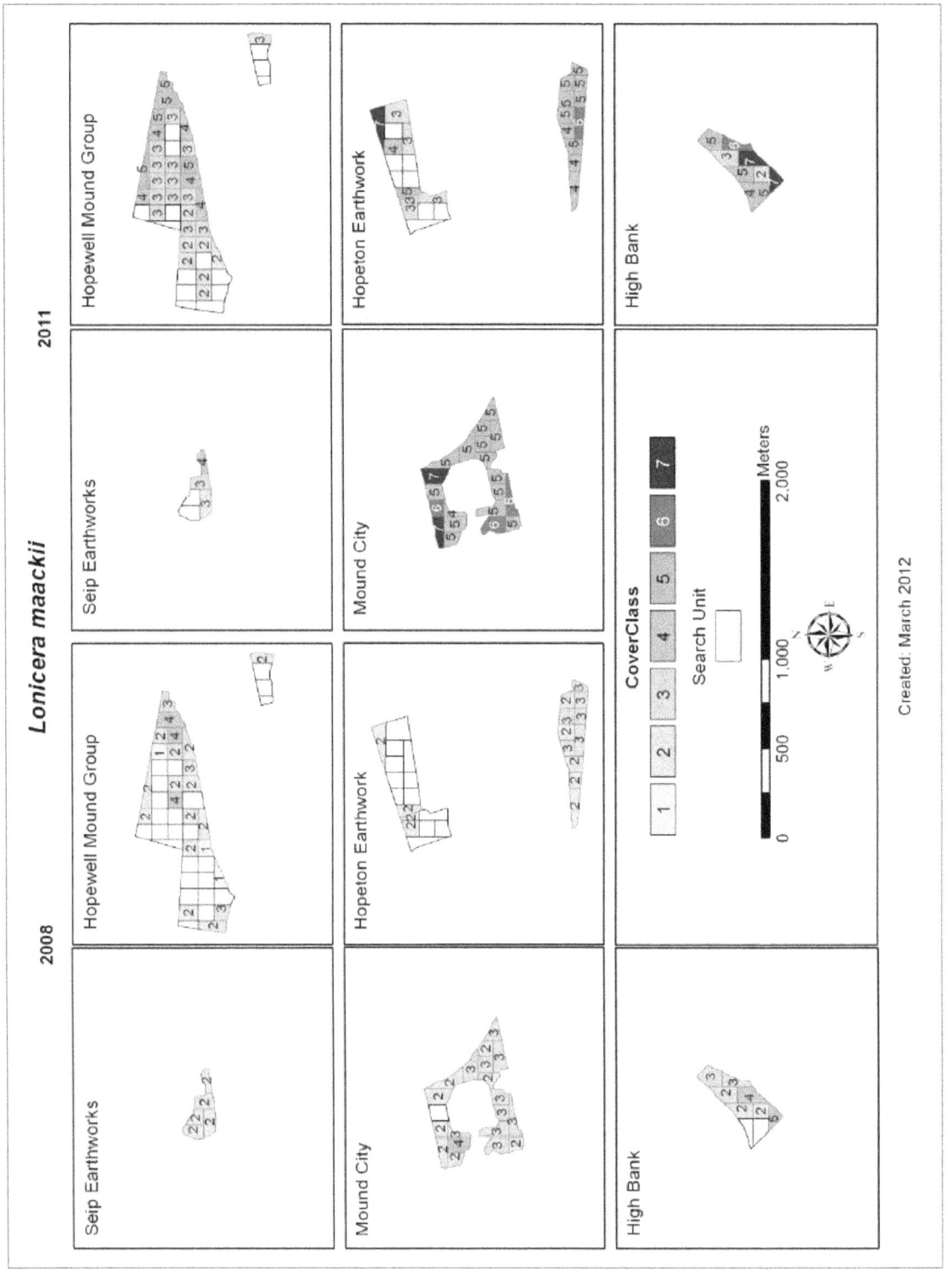

Figure 2. Abundance and distribution of *Lonicera macckii* (amur honeysuckle) at Hopewell Culture National Historical Park, 2008 and 2011. Cover classes are as follows: $1=0.1$-0.9 m^2, $2=1$-9.9 m^2, $3=10$-49.9 m^2, $4=50$-99.9 m^2, $5=100$-499.9 m^2, $6=500$-999.9 m^2, $7=1,000$-$4,999$ m^2.

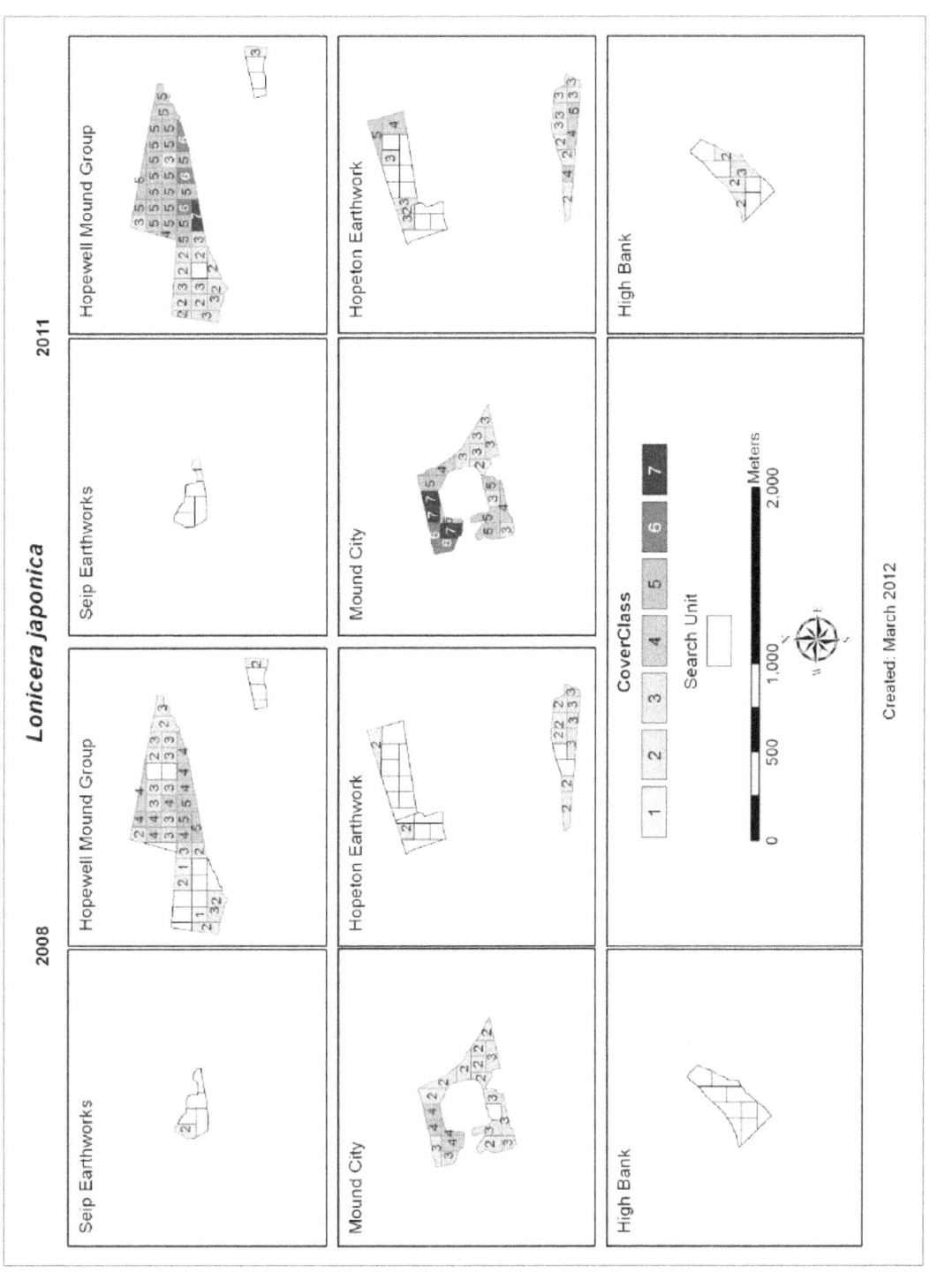

Figure 3. Abundance and distribution of *Lonicera japonica* (autumn olive) at Hopewell Culture National Historical Park, 2008 and 2011. Cover classes are as follows: 1=0.1-0.9 m^2, 2=1-9.9 m^2, 3=10-49.9 m^2, 4= 50-99.9 m^2, 5=100-499.9 m^2, 6= 500-999.9 m^2, 7= 1,000-4,999 m^2.

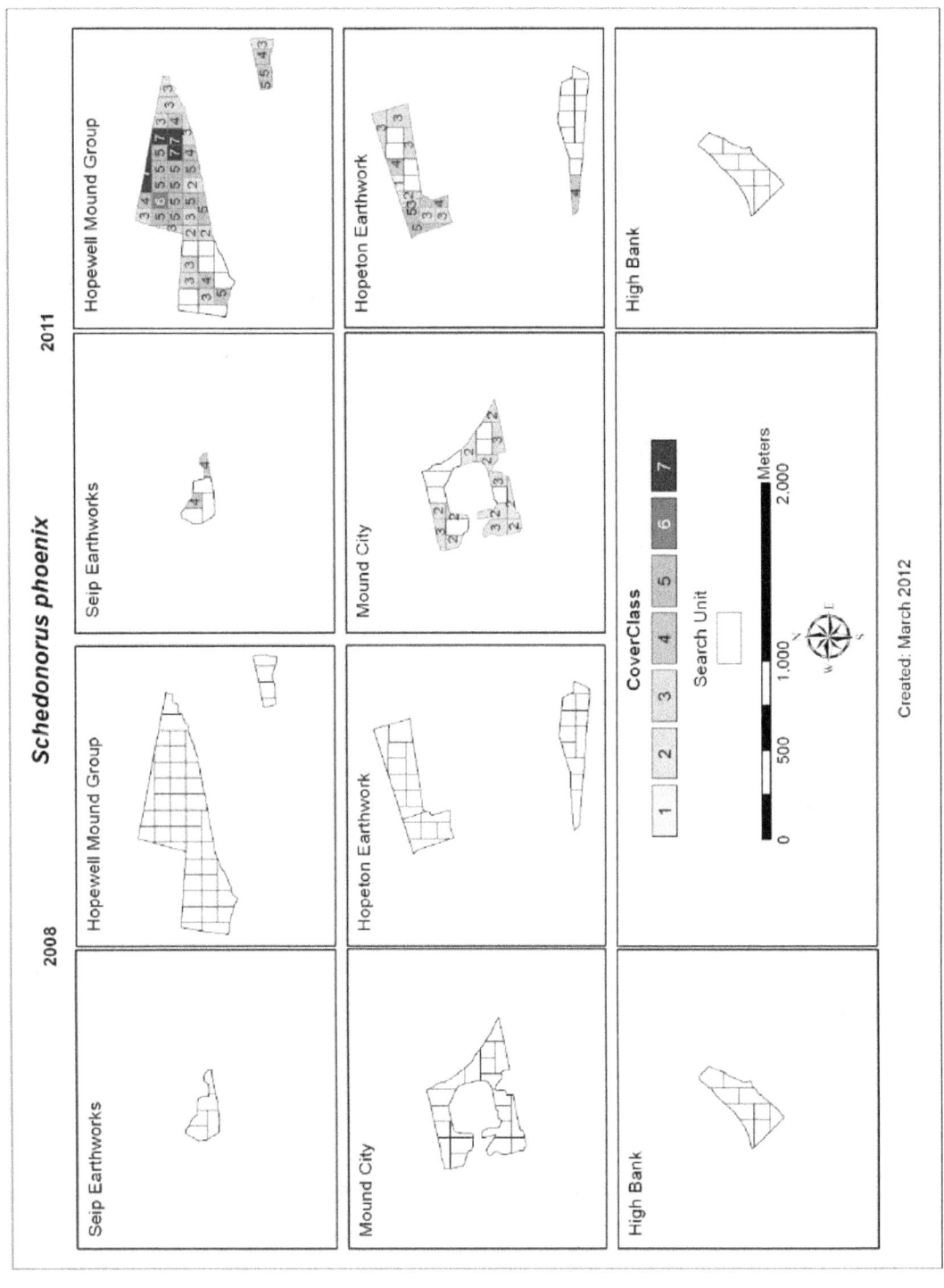

Figure 4. Abundance and distribution of *Schedonorus phonenix* (tall fescue) at Hopewell Culture National Historical Park, 2008 and 2011. Cover classes are as follows: 1=0.1-0.9 m², 2=1-9.9 m², 3=10-49.9 m², 4= 50-99.9 m², 5=100-499.9 m², 6= 500-999.9 m², 7= 1,000-4,999 m².

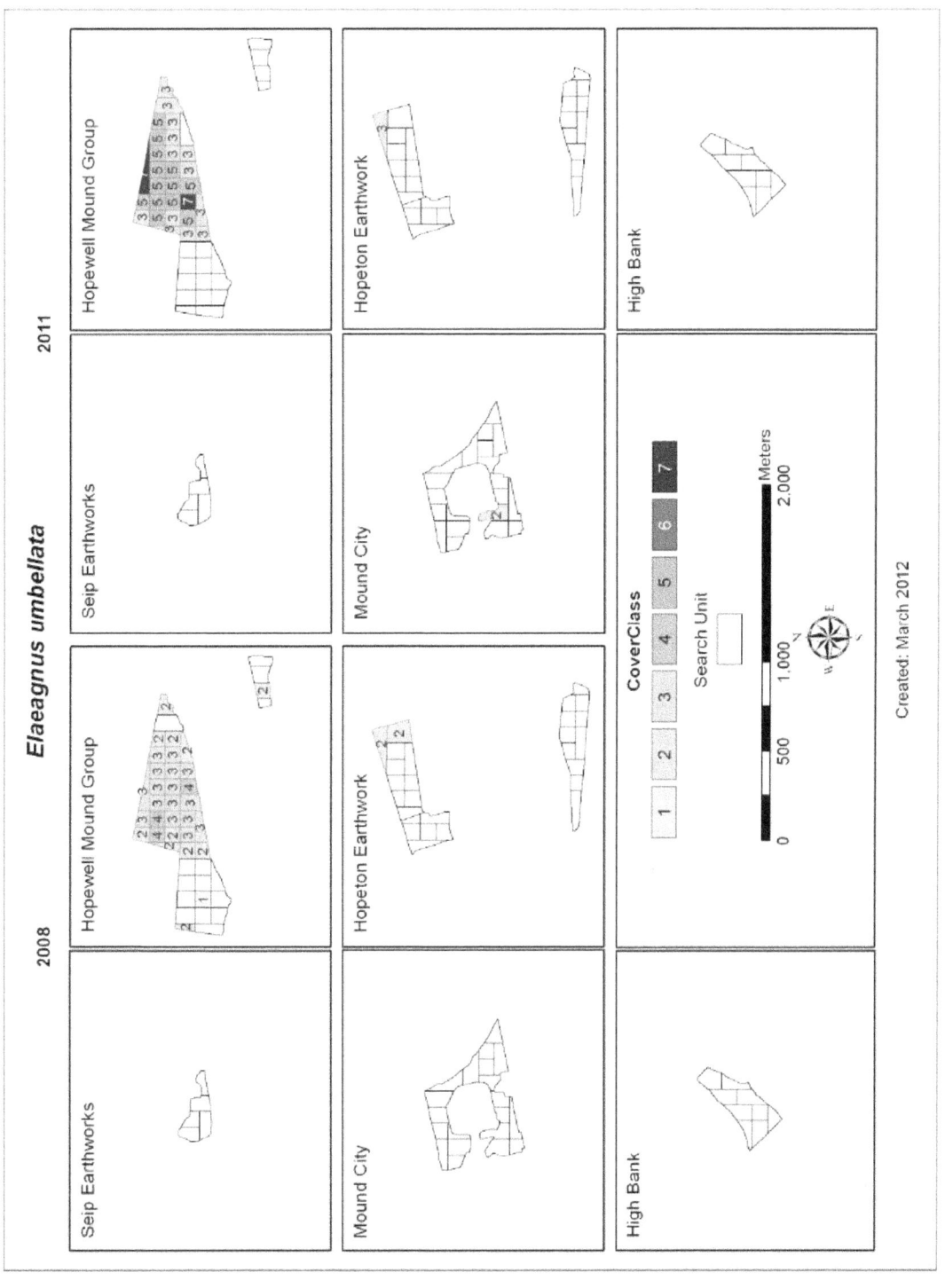

Figure 5. Abundance and distribution of *Elaeagnus umbellata* (autumn olive) at Hopewell Culture National Historical Park, 2008 and 2011. Cover classes are as follows: 1=0.1-0.9 m², 2=1-9.9 m², 3=10-49.9 m², 4= 50-99.9 m², 5=100-499.9 m², 6= 500-999.9 m², 7= 1,000-4,999 m².

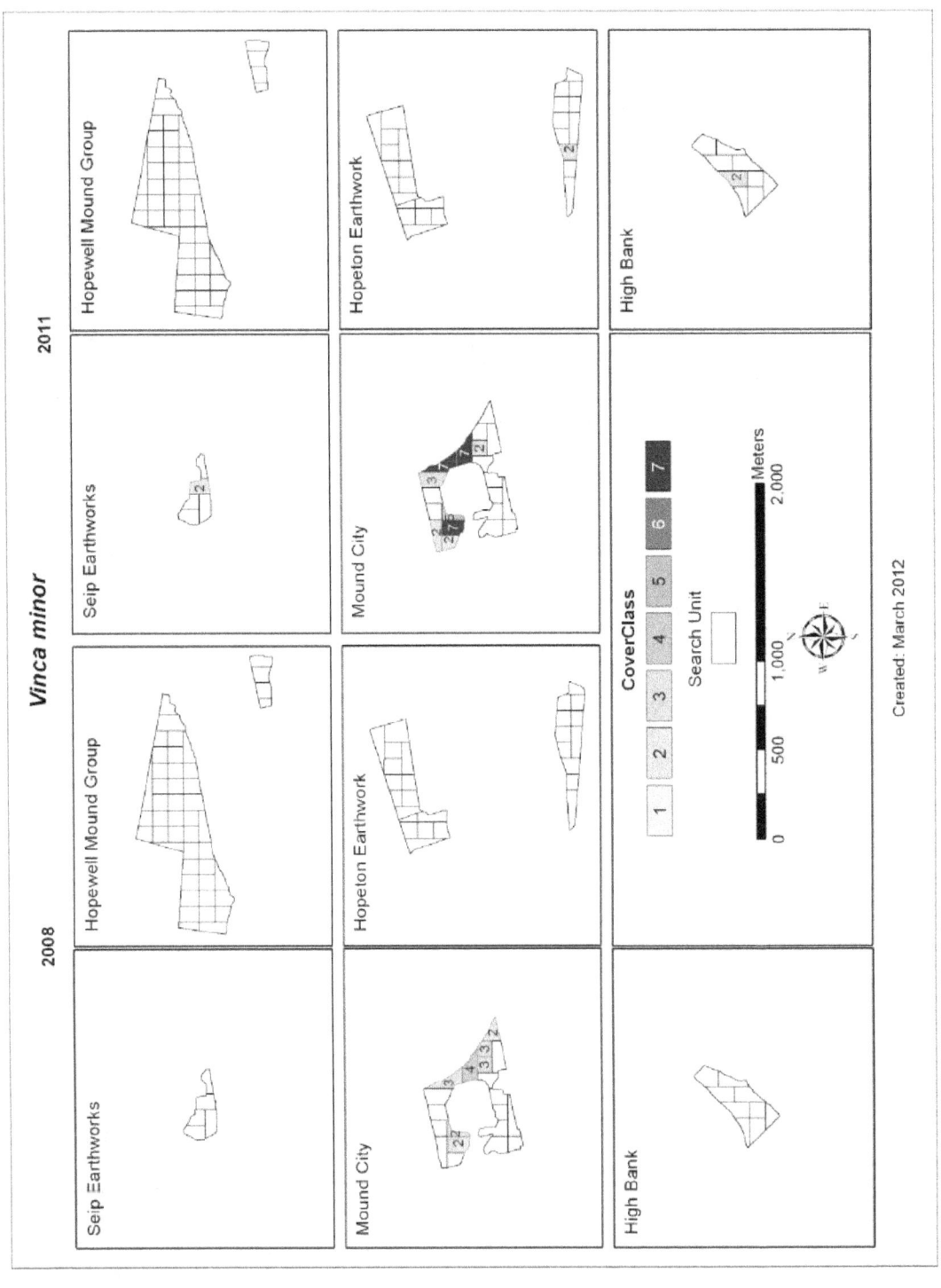

Figure 6. Abundance and distribution of *Vinca minor* (common periwinkle) at Hopewell Culture National Historical Park, 2008 and 2011. Cover classes are as follows: 1=0.1-0.9 m², 2=1-9.9 m², 3=10-49.9 m², 4= 50-99.9 m², 5=100-499.9 m², 6= 500-999.9 m², 7= 1,000-4,999 m².

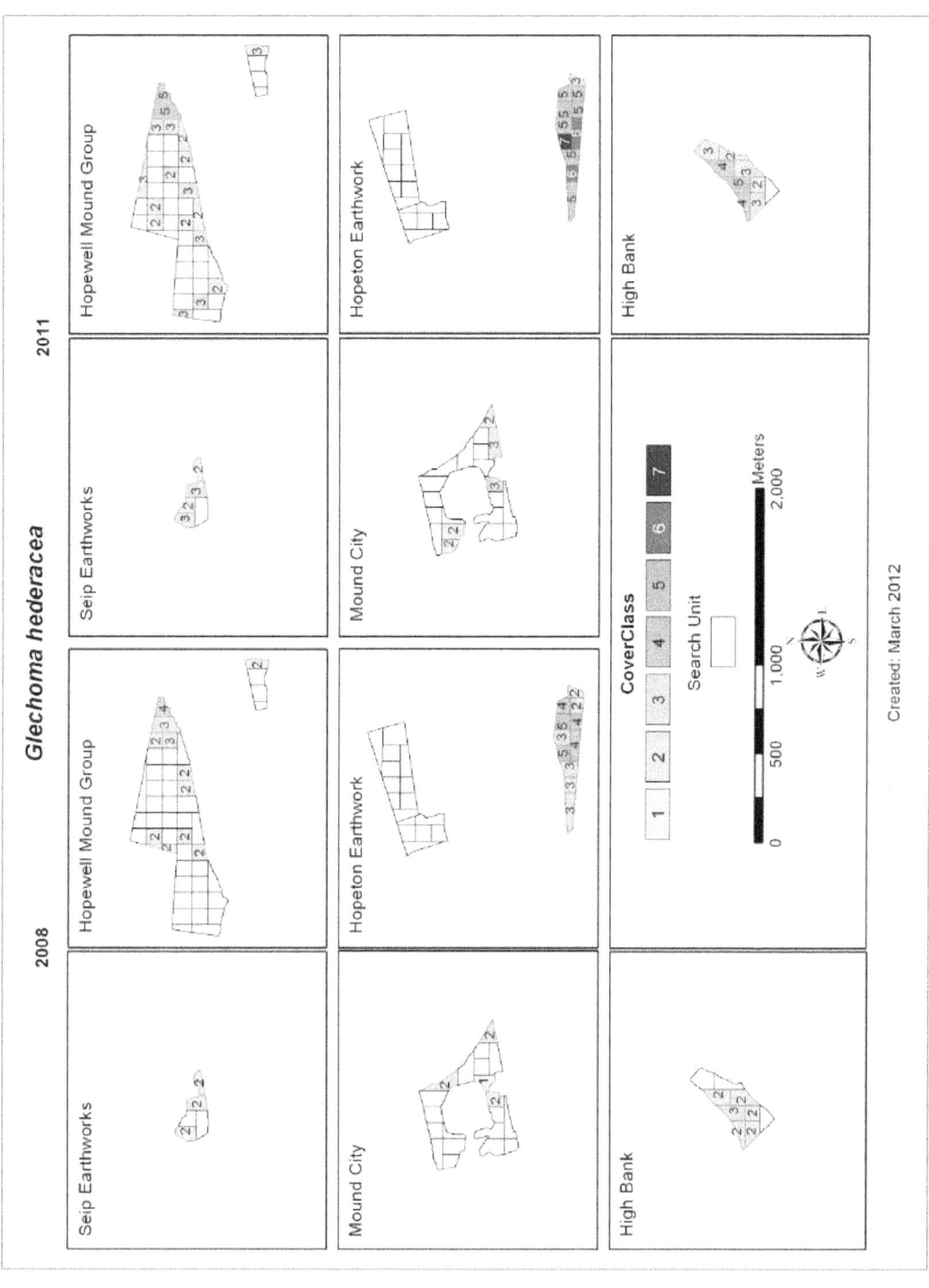

Figure 7. Abundance and distribution of *Glechoma hederacea* (ground ivy) at Hopewell Culture National Historical Park, 2008 and 2011. Cover classes are as follows: 1=0.1-0.9 m^2, 2=1-9.9 m^2, 3=10-49.9 m^2, 4= 50-99.9 m^2, 5=100-499.9 m^2, 6= 500-999.9 m^2, 7= 1,000-4,999 m^2.

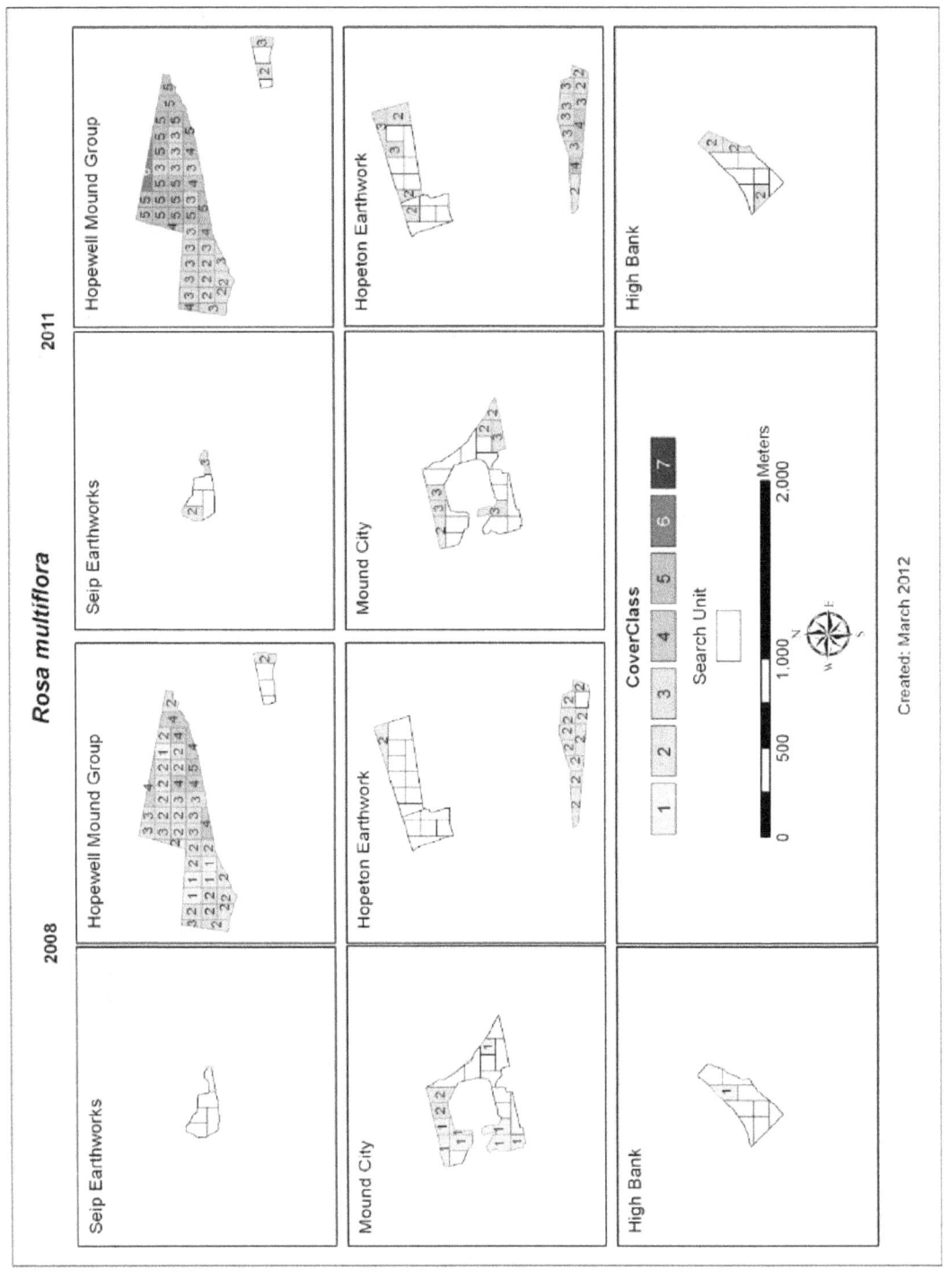

Figure 8. Abundance and distribution of *Rosa multiflora* (multiflora rose) at Hopewell Culture National Historical Park, 2008 and 2011. Cover classes are as follows: 1=0.1-0.9 m^2, 2=1-9.9 m^2, 3=10-49.9 m^2, 4= 50-99.9 m^2, 5=100-499.9 m^2, 6= 500-999.9 m^2, 7= 1,000-4,999 m^2.

18

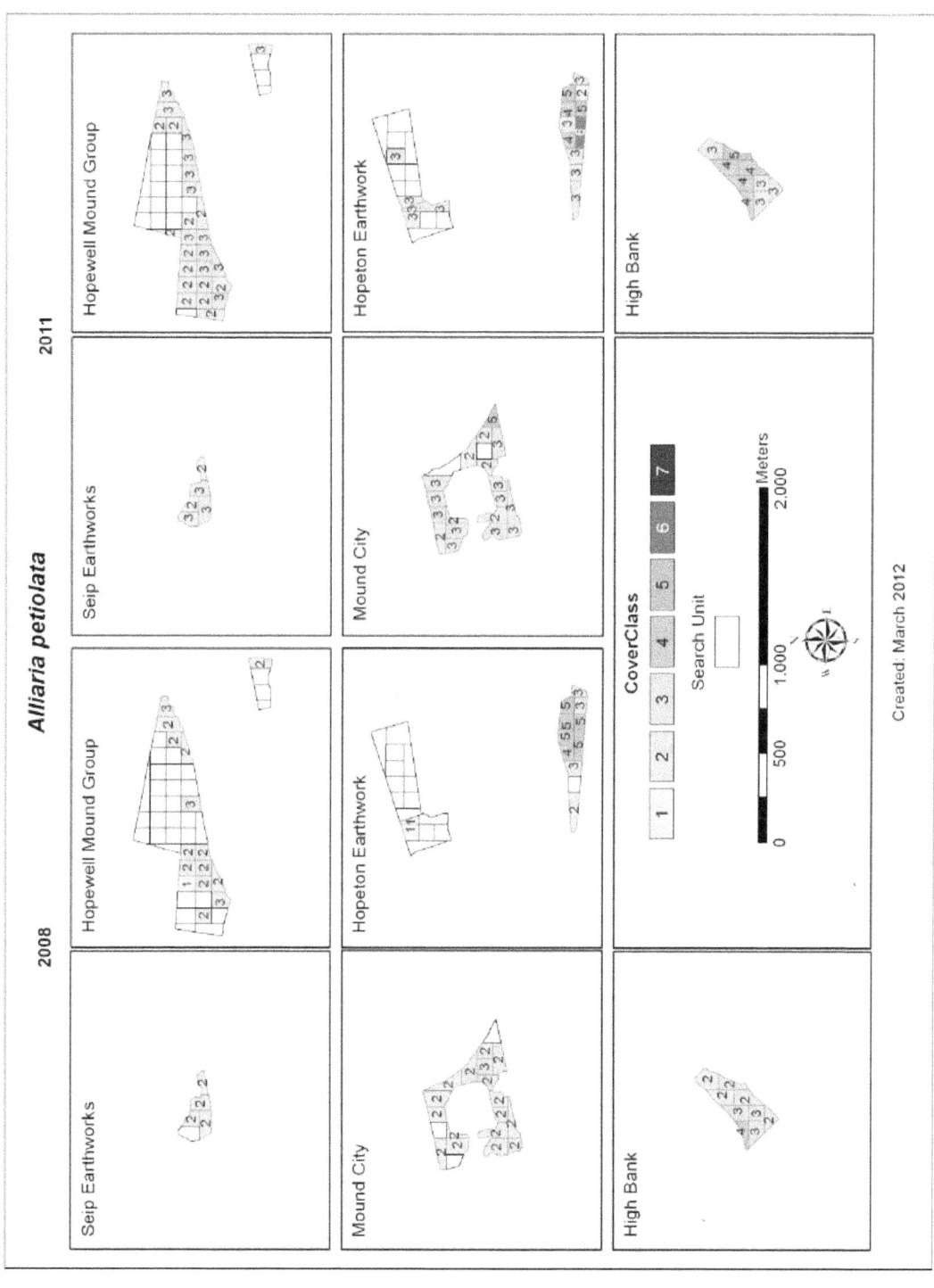

Figure 9. Abundance and distribution of *Alliaria petiolata* (garlic mustard) at Hopewell Culture National Historical Park, 2008 and 2011. Cover classes are as follows: 1=0.1-0.9 m², 2=1-9.9 m², 3=10-49.9 m², 4= 50-99.9 m², 5=100-499.9 m², 6= 500-999.9 m², 7= 1,000-4,999 m².

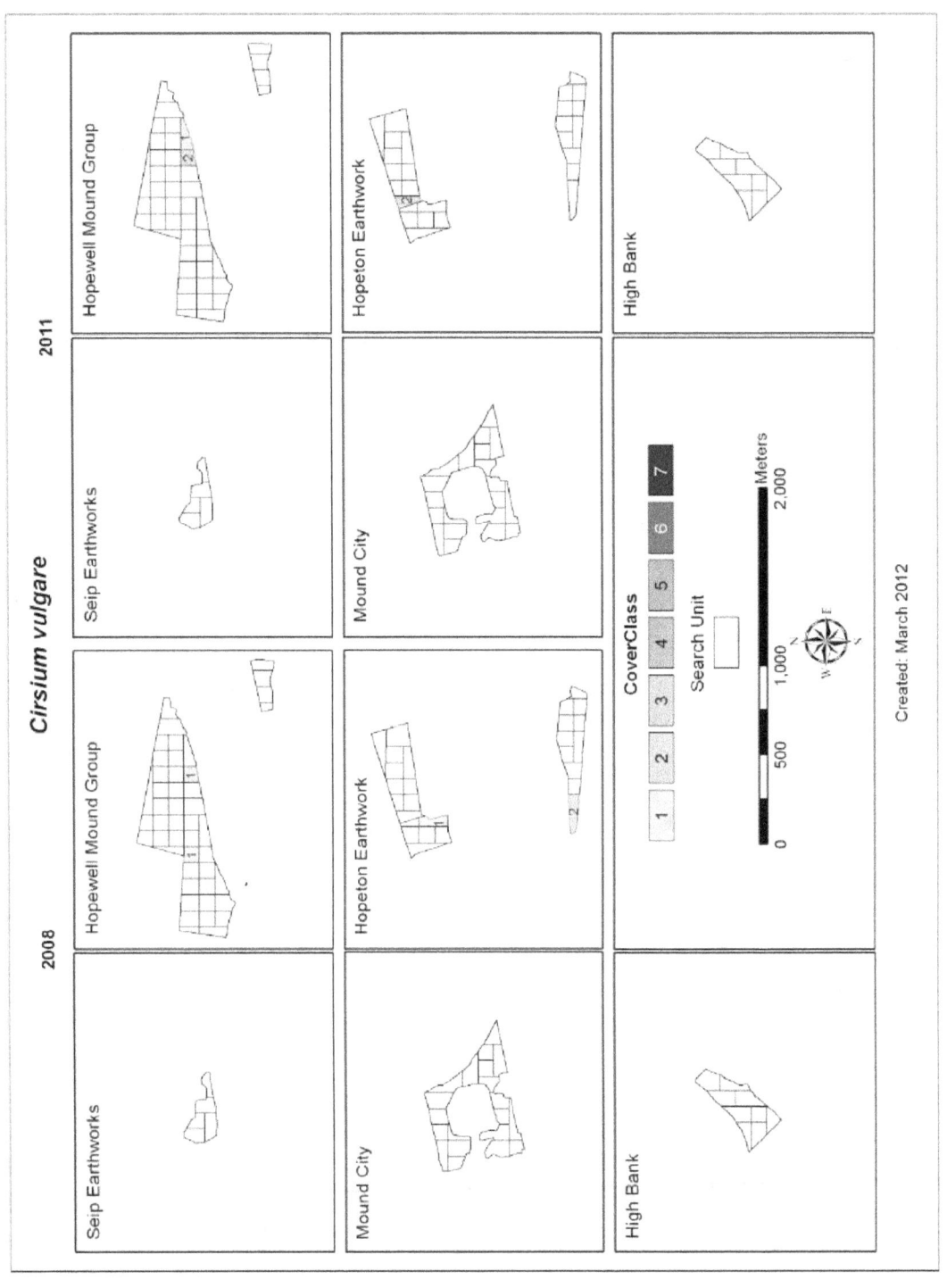

Figure 10. Abundance and distribution of *Cirsium vulgare* (bull thistle) at Hopewell Culture National Historical Park, 2008 and 2011. Cover classes are as follows: 1=0.1-0.9 m^2, 2=1-9.9 m^2, 3=10-49.9 m^2, 4= 50-99.9 m^2, 5=100-499.9 m^2, 6= 500-999.9 m^2, 7= 1,000-4,999 m^2.

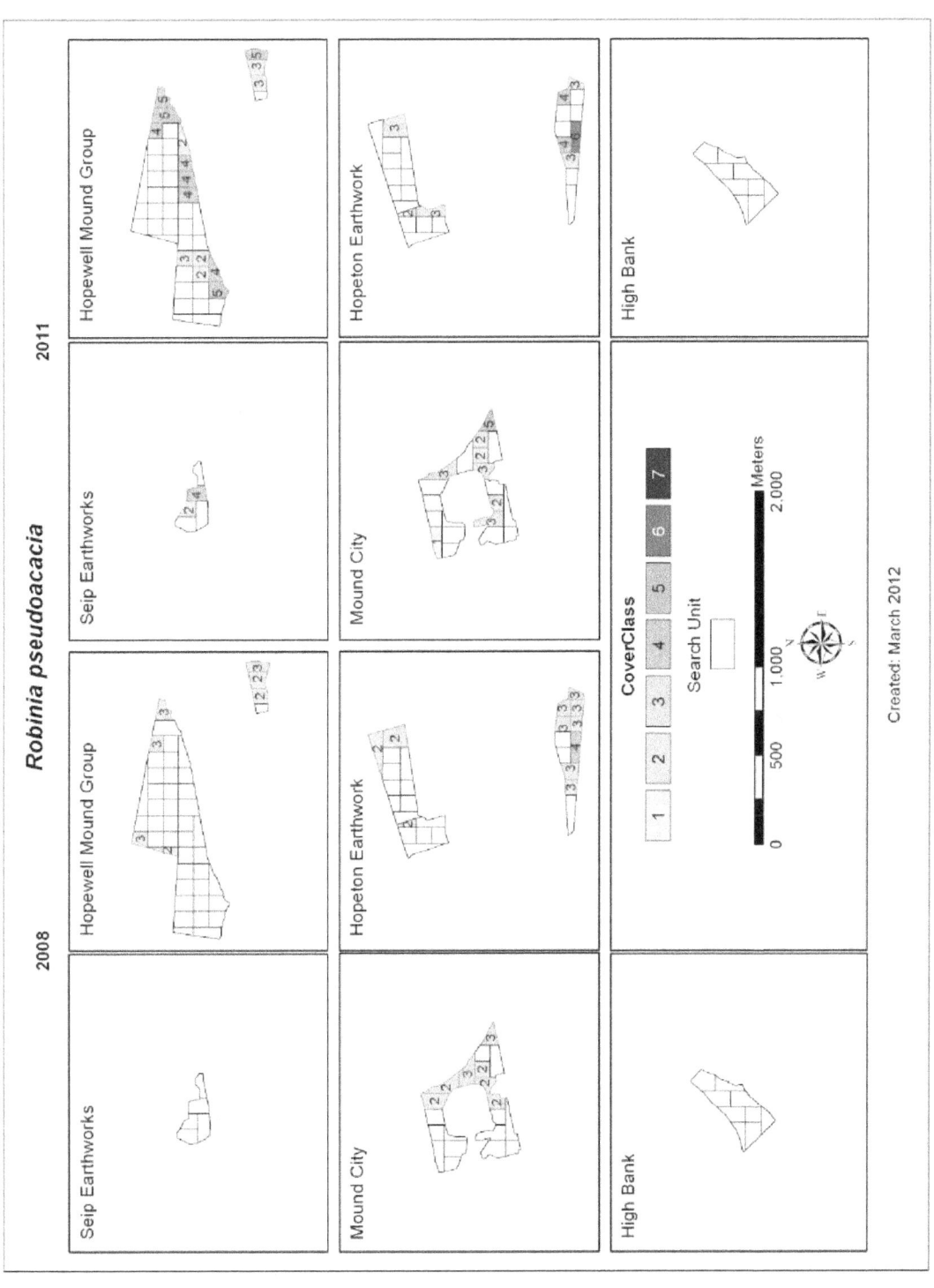

Figure 11. Abundance and distribution of *Robinia pseudoacacia* (black locust) at Hopewell Culture National Historical Park, 2008 and 2011. Cover classes are as follows: 1=0.1-0.9 m², 2=1-9.9 m², 3=10-49.9 m², 4= 50-99.9 m², 5=100-499.9 m², 6= 500-999.9 m², 7= 1,000-4,999 m².

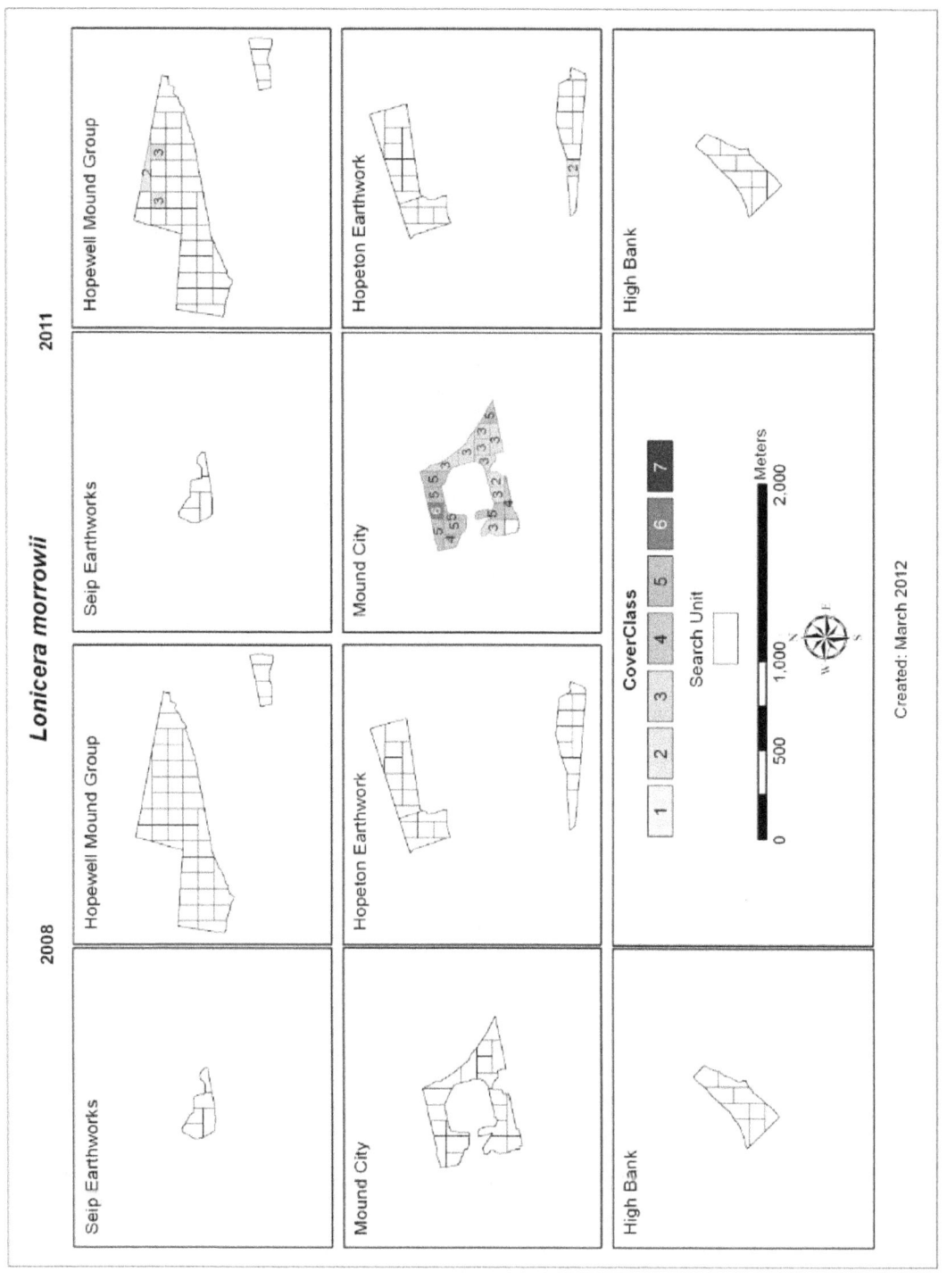

Figure 12. Abundance and distribution of *Lonicera morrowii* (Morrow's honeysuckle) at Hopewell Culture National Historical Park, 2008 and 2011. Cover classes are as follows: $1 = 0.1\text{-}0.9 \text{ m}^2$, $2 = 1\text{-}9.9 \text{ m}^2$, $3 = 10\text{-}49.9 \text{ m}^2$, $4 = 50\text{-}99.9 \text{ m}^2$, $5 = 100\text{-}499.9 \text{ m}^2$, $6 = 500\text{-}999.9 \text{ m}^2$, $7 = 1,000\text{-}4,999 \text{ m}^2$.

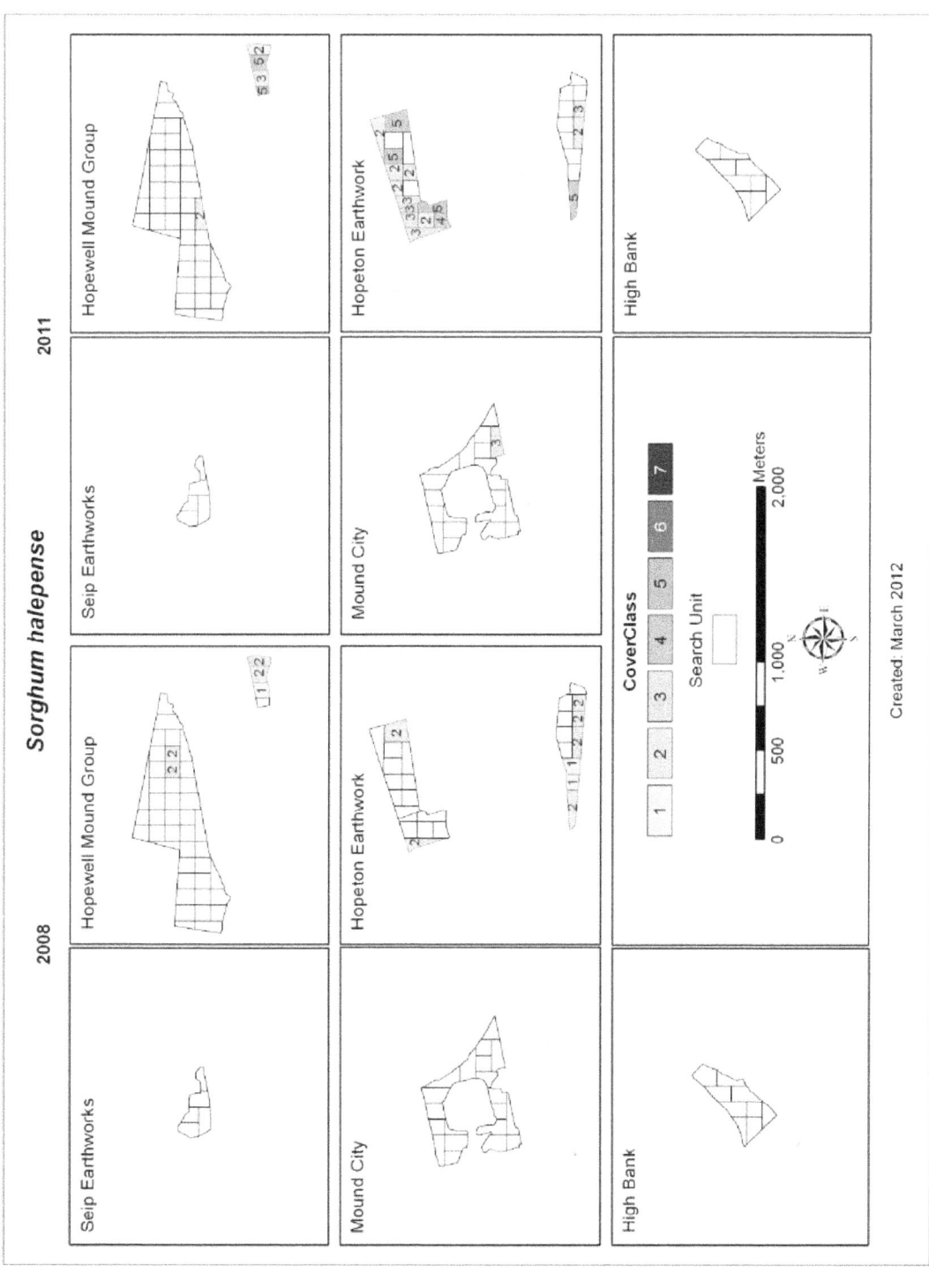

Figure 13. Abundance and distribution of *Sorghum halepense* (Johnsongrass) at Hopewell Culture National Historical Park, 2008 and 2011. Cover classes are as follows: 1=0.1-0.9 m2, 2=1-9.9 m2, 3=10-49.9 m2, 4= 50-99.9 m2, 5=100-499.9 m2, 6= 500-999.9 m2, 7= 1,000-4,999 m2.

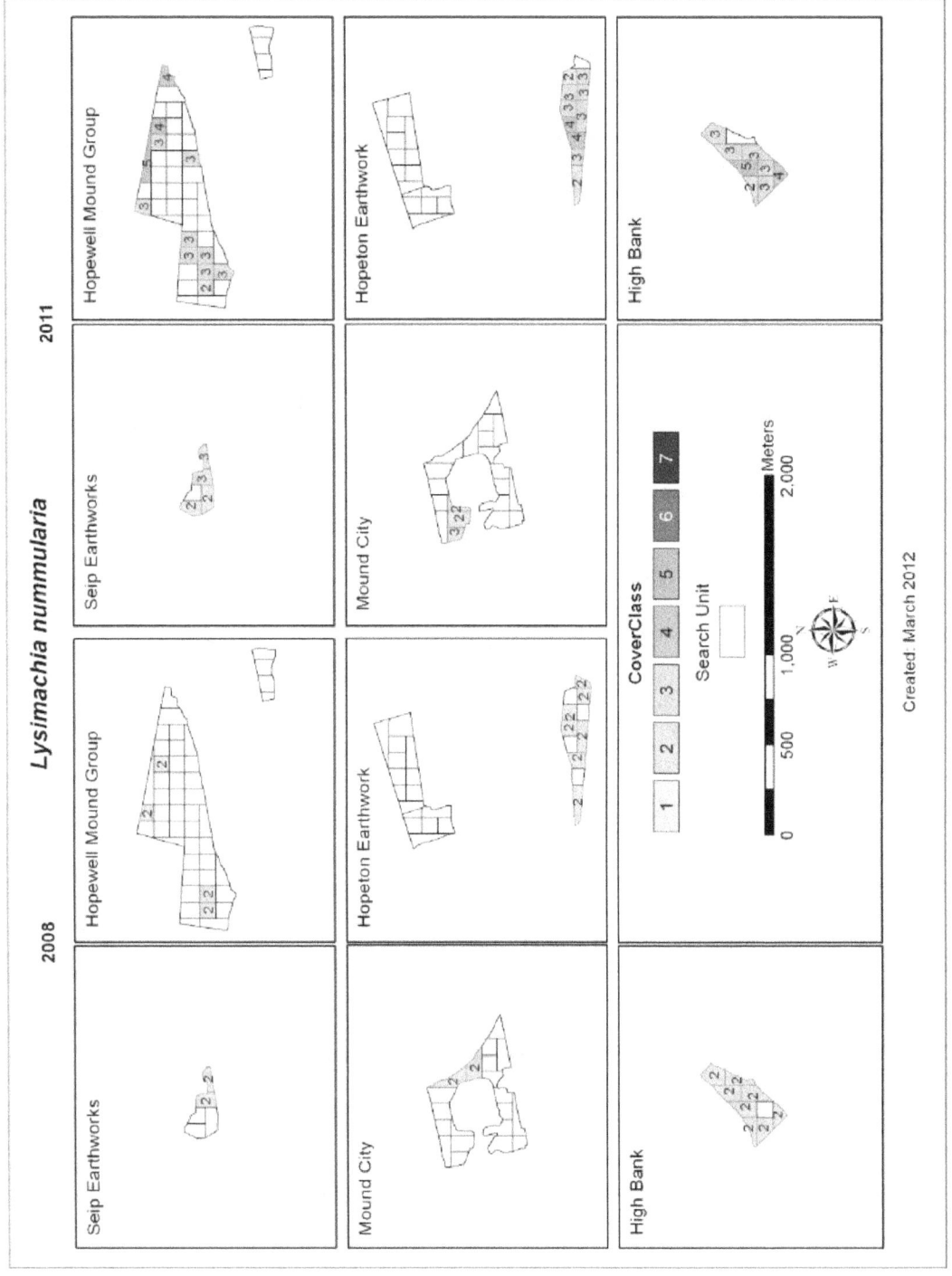

Figure 14. Abundance and distribution of *Lysimachia nummularia* (creeping jenny) at Hopewell Culture National Historical Park, 2008 and 2011. Cover classes are as follows: 1=0.1-0.9 m², 2=1-9.9 m², 3=10-49.9 m², 4= 50-99.9 m², 5=100-499.9 m², 6= 500-999.9 m², 7= 1,000-4,999 m².

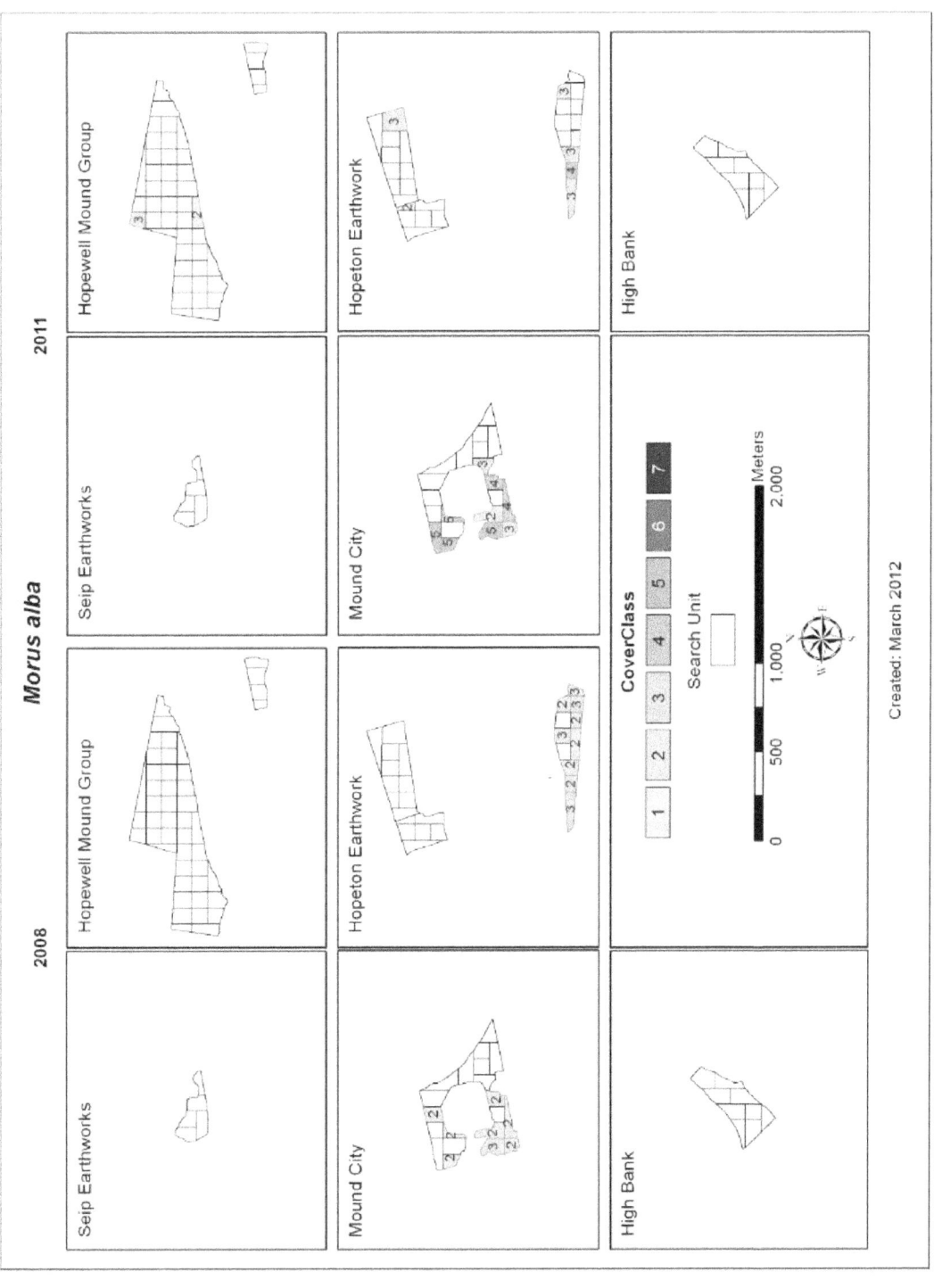

Figure 15. Abundance and distribution of *Morus alba* (white mulberry) at Hopewell Culture National Historical Park, 2008 and 2011. Cover classes are as follows: 1=0.1-0.9 m^2, 2=1-9.9 m^2, 3=10-49.9 m^2, 4= 50-99.9 m^2, 5=100-499.9 m^2, 6= 500-999.9 m^2, 7= 1,000-4,999 m^2.

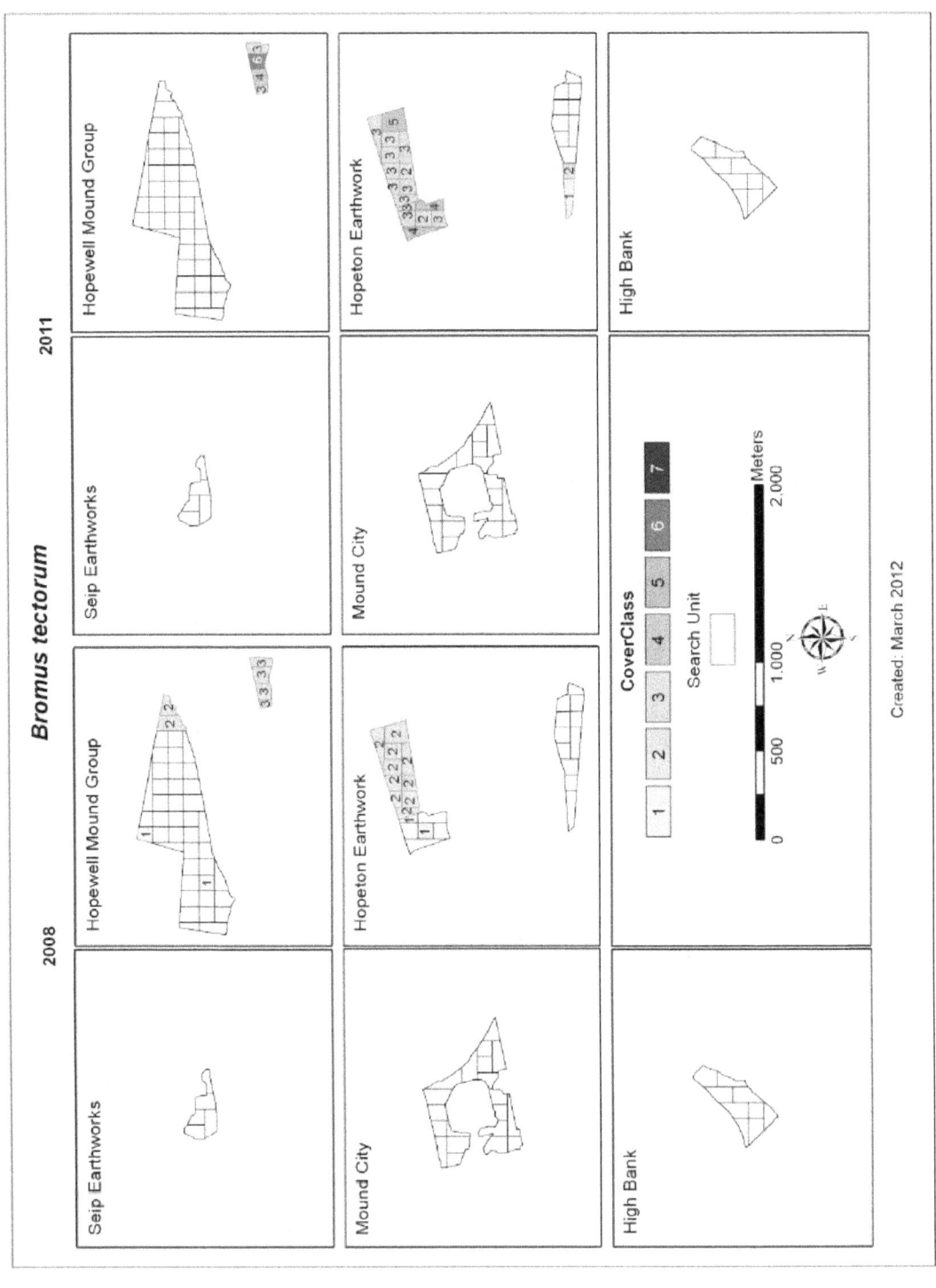

Figure 16. Abundance and distribution of *Bromus tectorum* (cheatgrass) at Hopewell Culture National Historical Park, 2008 and 2011. Cover classes are as follows: 1=0.1-0.9 m^2, 2=1-9.9 m^2, 3=10-49.9 m^2, 4= 50-99.9 m^2, 5=100-499.9 m^2, 6= 500-999.9 m^2, 7= 1,000-4,999 m^2.

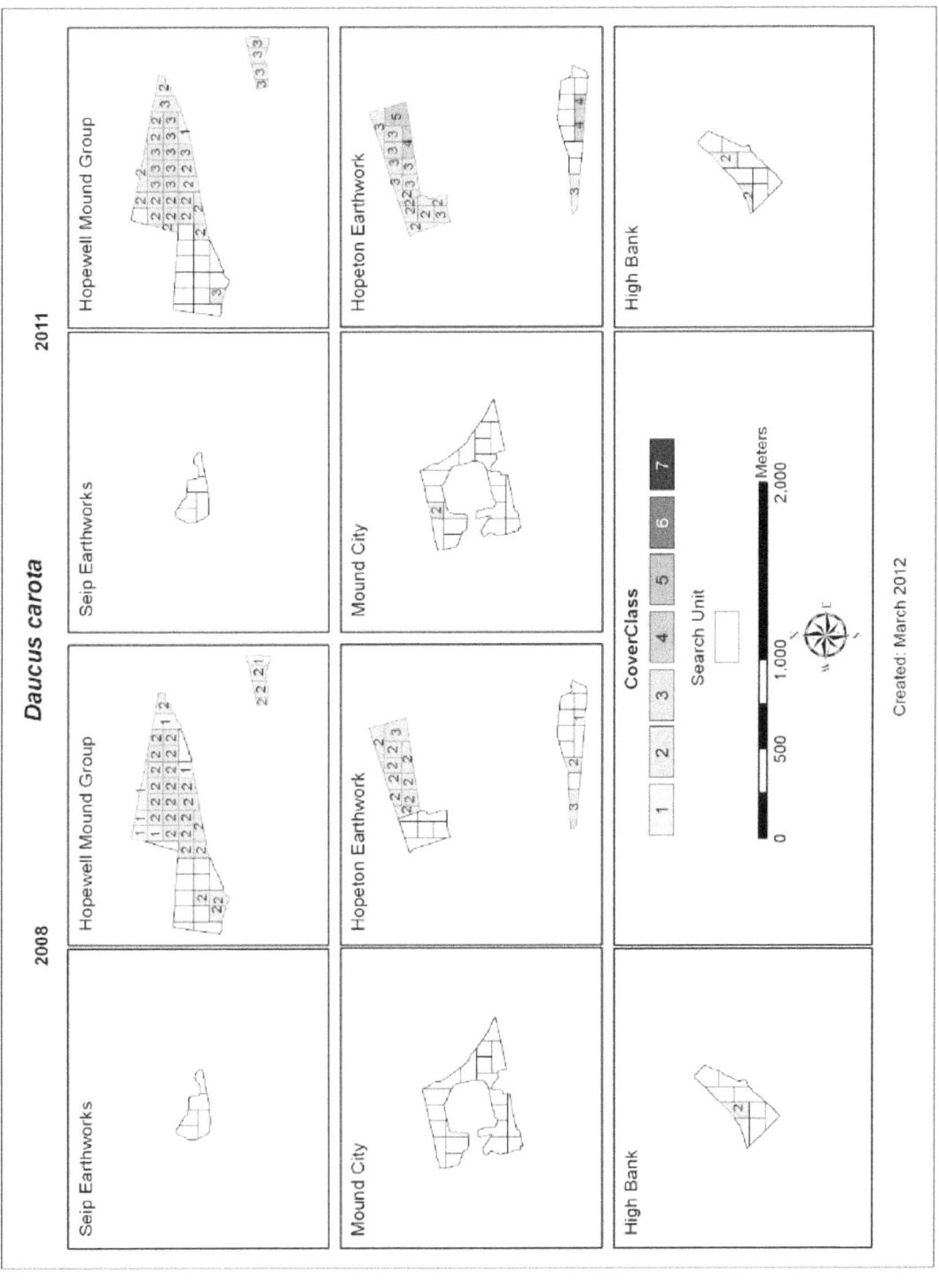

Figure 17. Abundance and distribution of *Daucus carota* (Queen Anne's lace) at Hopewell Culture National Historical Park, 2008 and 2011. Cover classes are as follows: 1=0.1-0.9 m², 2=1-9.9 m², 3=10-49.9 m², 4= 50-99.9 m², 5=100-499.9 m², 6= 500-999.9 m², 7= 1,000-4,999 m².

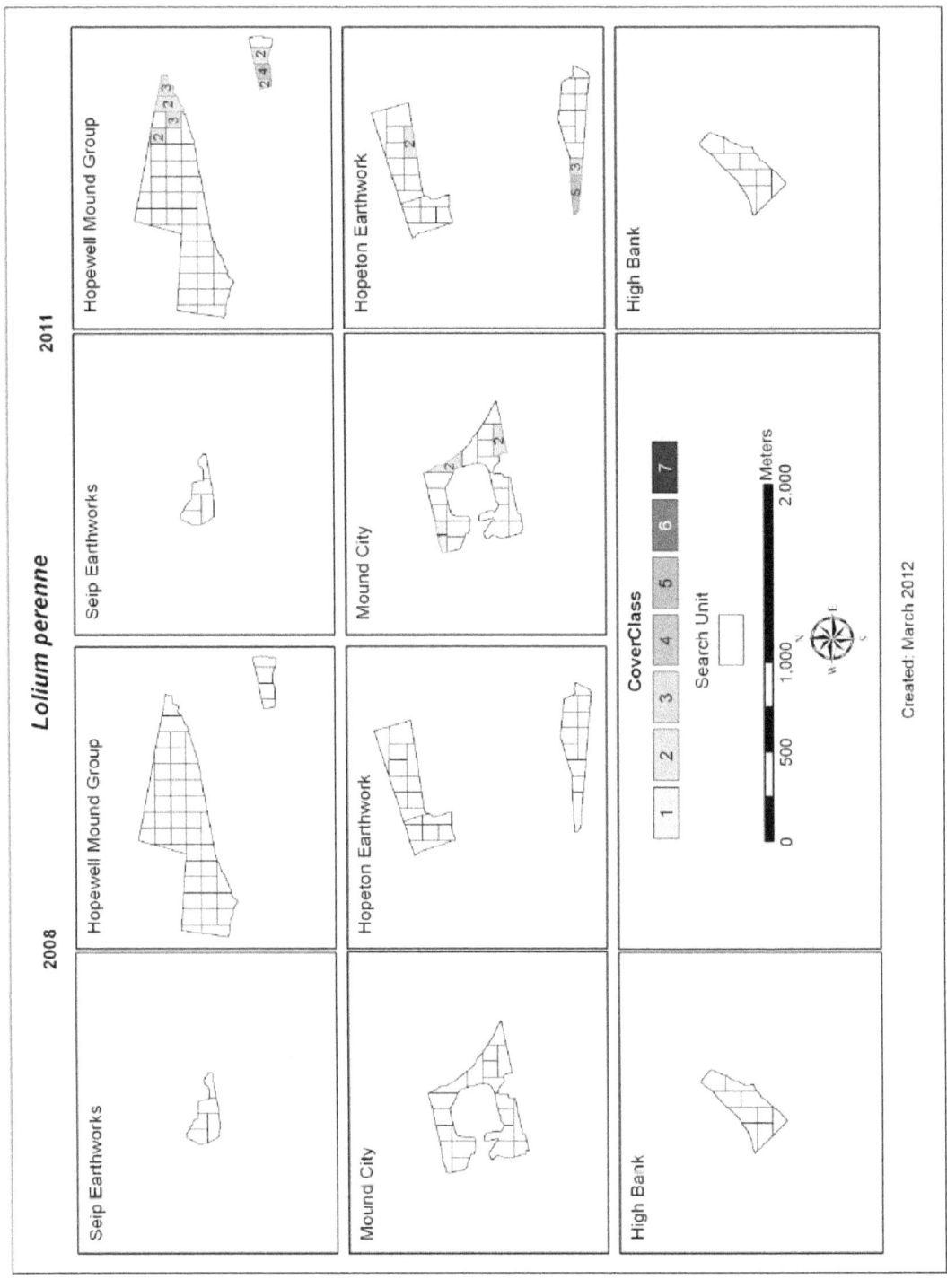

Figure 18. Abundance and distribution of *Lolium perenne* (perennial ryegrass) at Hopewell Culture National Historical Park, 2008 and 2011. Cover classes are as follows: 1=0.1-0.9 m^2, 2=1-9.9 m^2, 3=10-49.9 m^2, 4= 50-99.9 m^2, 5=100-499.9 m^2, 6= 500-999.9 m^2, 7= 1,000-4,999 m^2.

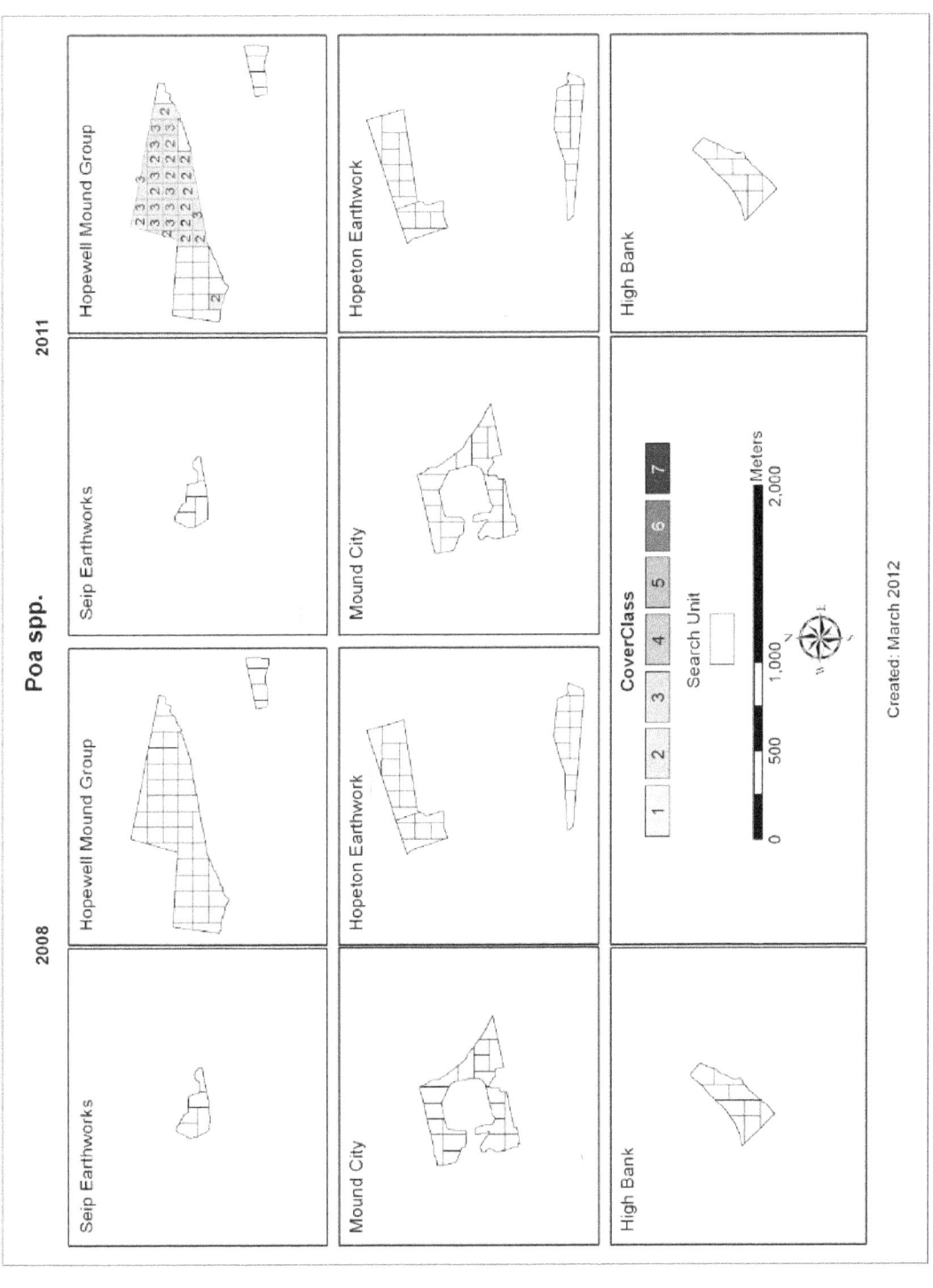

Figure 19. Abundance and distribution of *Poa* spp. (bluegrass) at Hopewell Culture National Historical Park, 2008 and 2011. Cover classes are as follows: $1=0.1-0.9$ m^2, $2=1-9.9$ m^2, $3=10-49.9$ m^2, $4=50-99.9$ m^2, $5=100-499.9$ m^2, $6=500-999.9$ m^2, $7=1,000-4,999$ m^2.

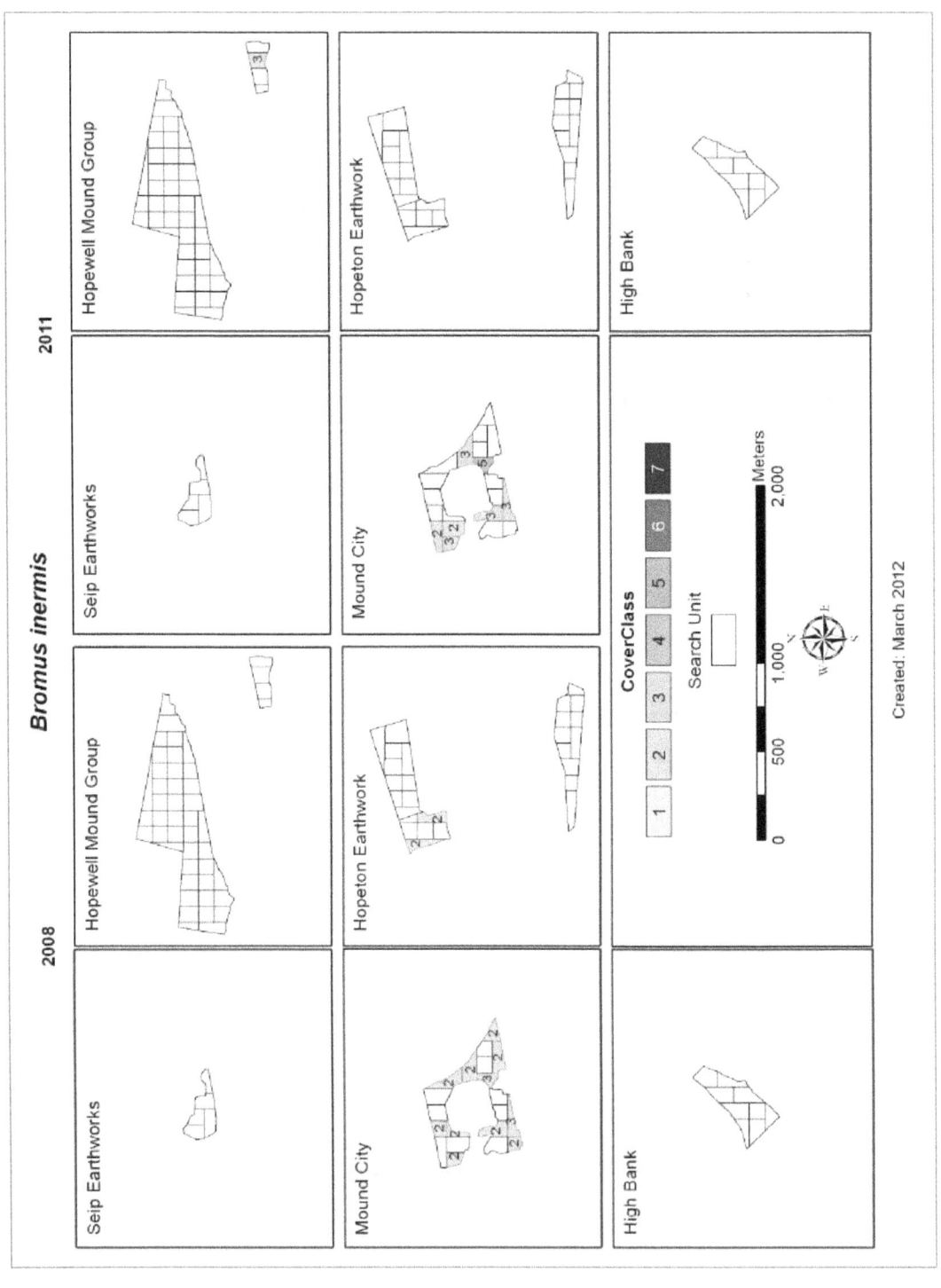

Figure 20. Abundance and distribution of *Bromus inermis* (smooth brome) at Hopewell Culture National Historical Park, 2008 and 2011. Cover classes are as follows: 1=0.1-0.9 m², 2=1-9.9 m², 3=10-49.9 m², 4= 50-99.9 m², 5=100-499.9 m², 6= 500-999.9 m², 7= 1,000-4,999 m².

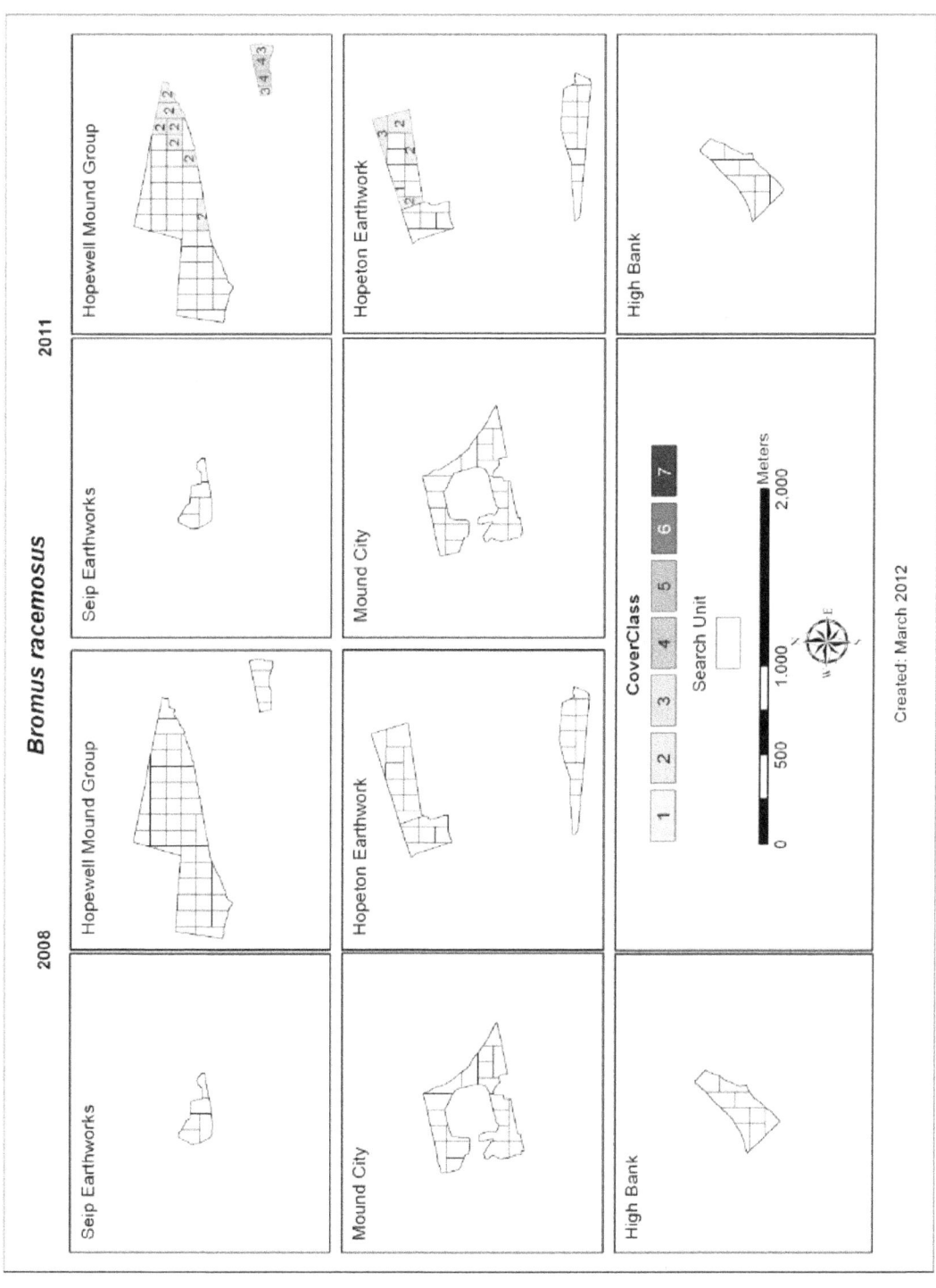

Figure 21. Abundance and distribution of *Bromus racemosus* (bald brome) at Hopewell Culture National Historical Park, 2008 and 2011. Cover classes are as follows: 1=0.1-0.9 m², 2=1-9.9 m², 3=10-49.9 m², 4= 50-99.9 m², 5=100-499.9 m², 6= 500-999.9 m², 7= 1,000-4,999 m².

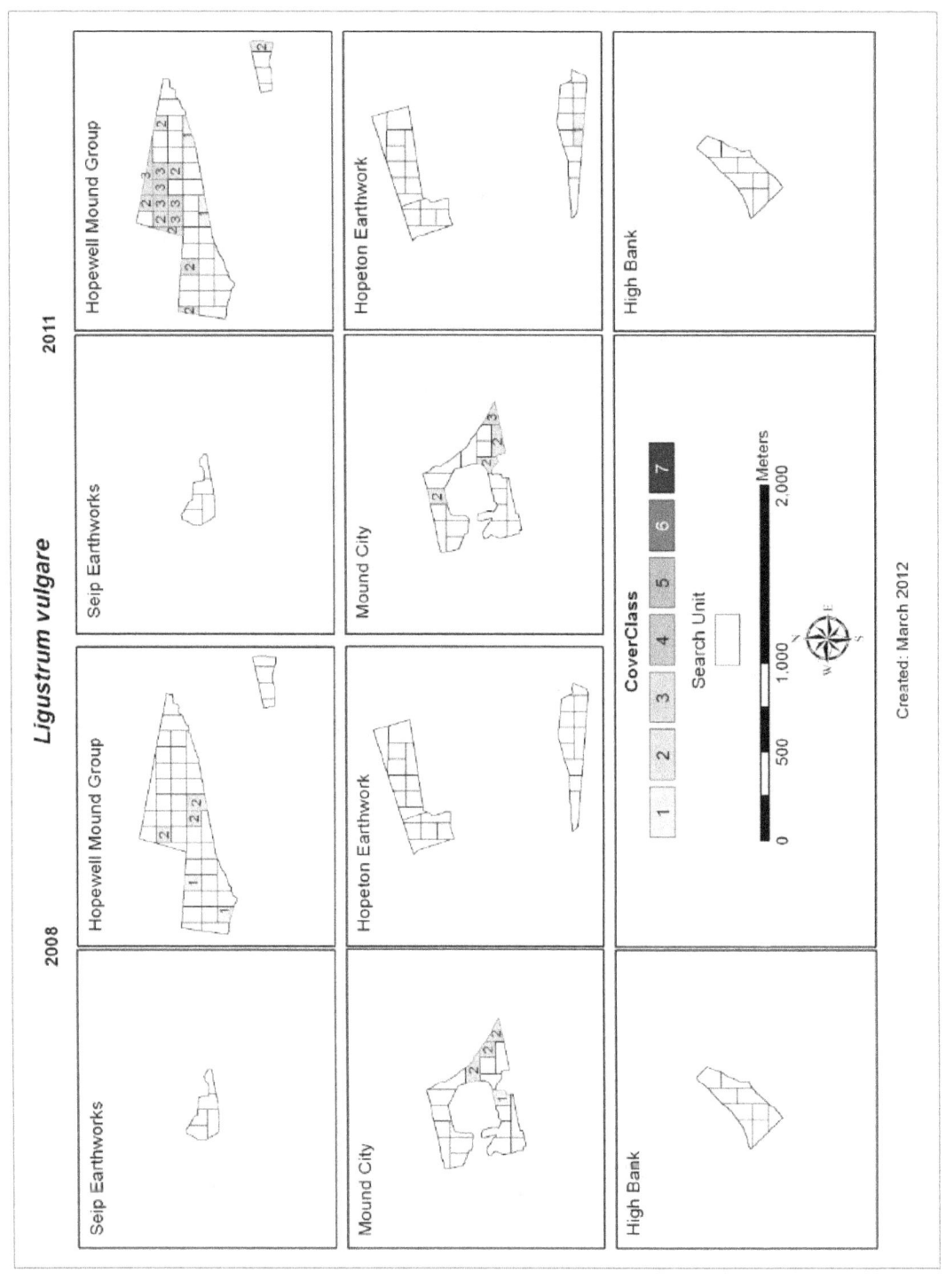

Figure 22. Abundance and distribution of *Ligustrum vulgare* (common privet) at Hopewell Culture National Historical Park, 2008 and 2011. Cover classes are as follows: 1=0.1-0.9 m², 2=1-9.9 m², 3=10-49.9 m², 4= 50-99.9 m², 5=100-499.9 m², 6= 500-999.9 m², 7= 1,000-4,999 m².

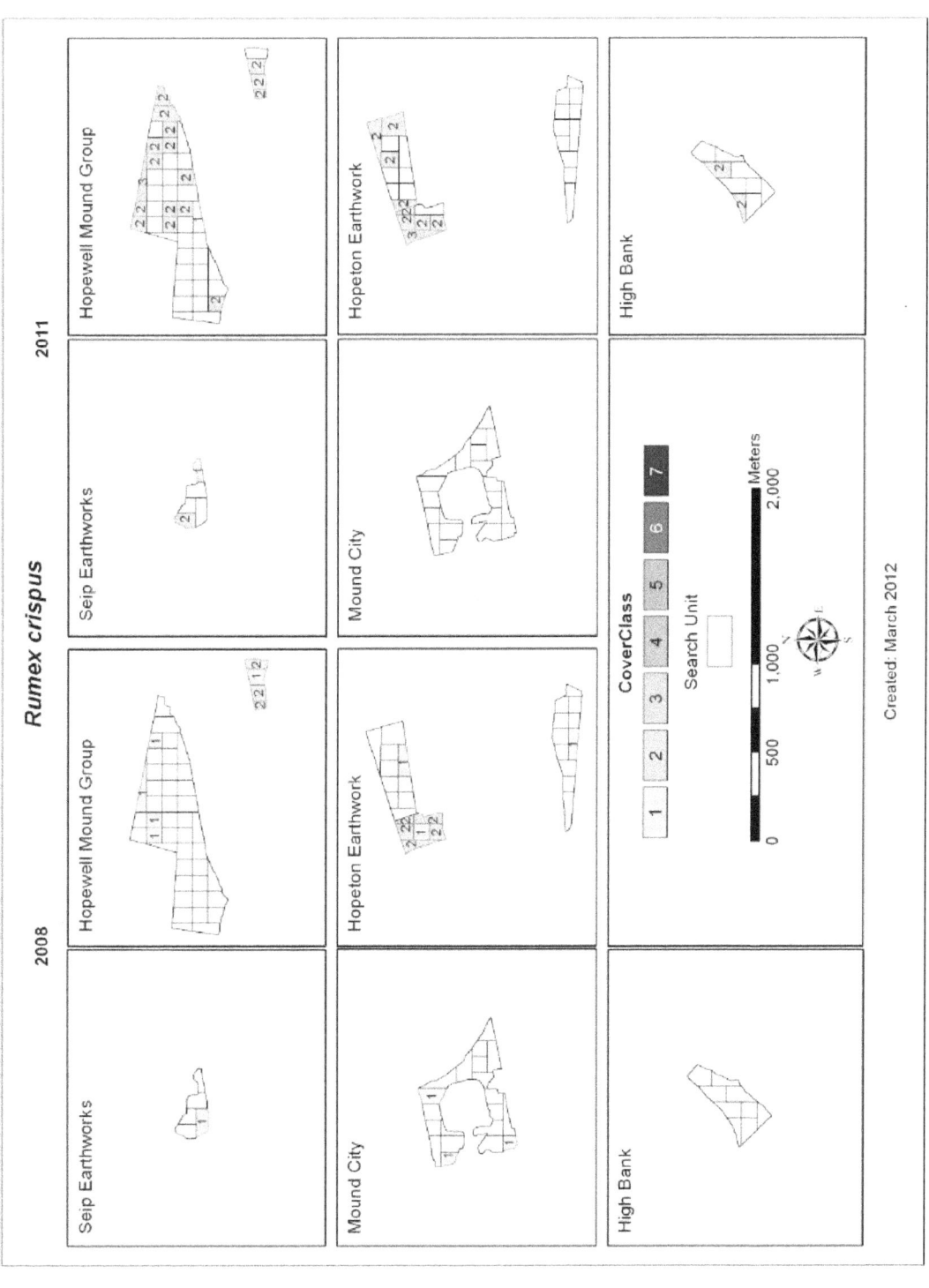

Figure 23. Abundance and distribution of *Rumex crispus* (curly dock) at Hopewell Culture National Historical Park, 2008 and 2011. Cover classes are as follows: 1=0.1-0.9 m², 2=1-9.9 m², 3=10-49.9 m², 4= 50-99.9 m², 5=100-499.9 m², 6= 500-999.9 m², 7= 1,000-4,999 m².

33

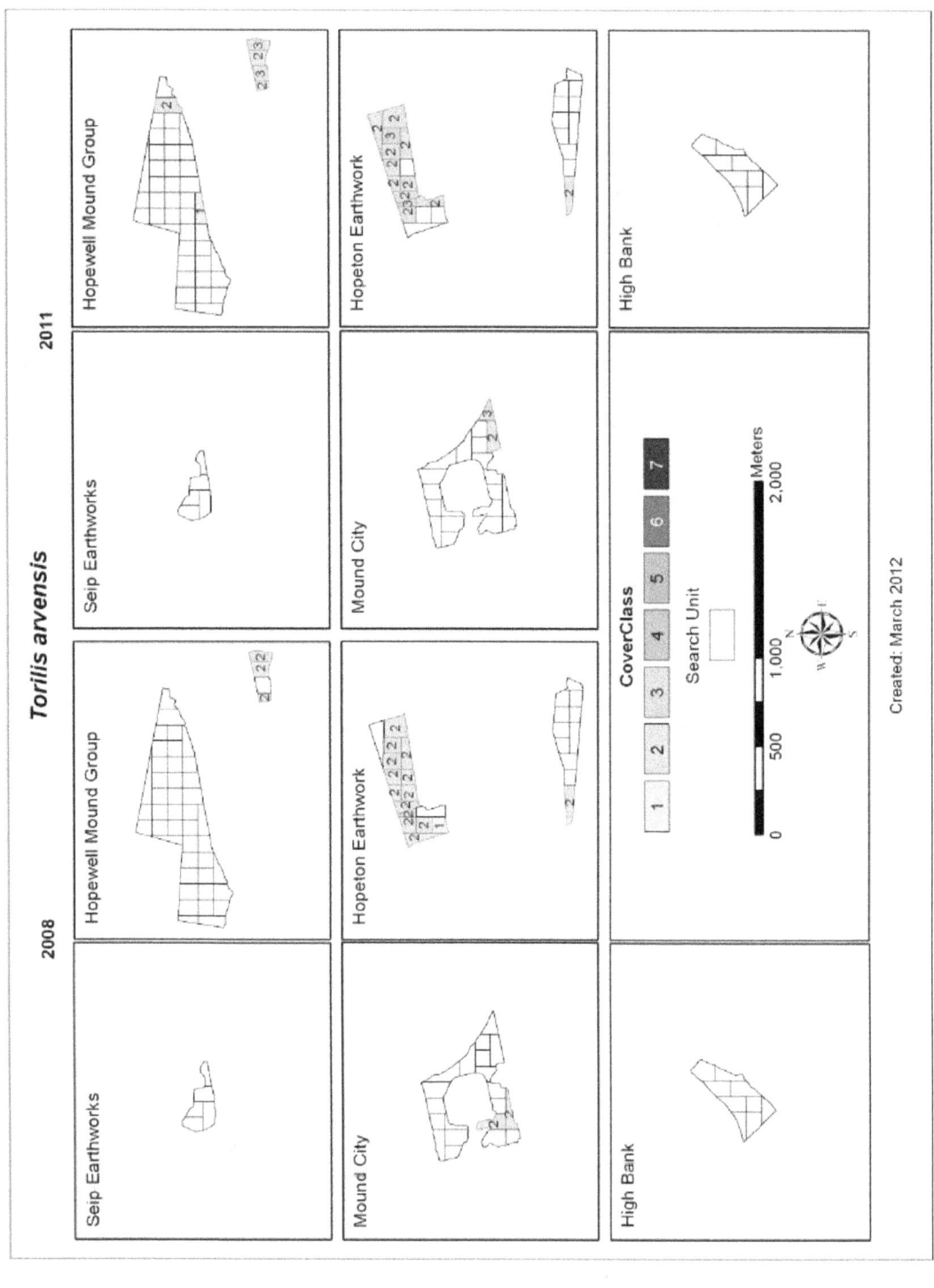

Figure 24. Abundance and distribution of *Torilis arvensis* (spreading hedgeparsley) at Hopewell Culture National Historical Park, 2008 and 2011. Cover classes are as follows: 1=0.1-0.9 m^2, 2=1-9.9 m^2, 3=10-49.9 m^2, 4= 50-99.9 m^2, 5=100-499.9 m^2, 6= 500-999.9 m^2, 7= 1,000-4,999 m^2.

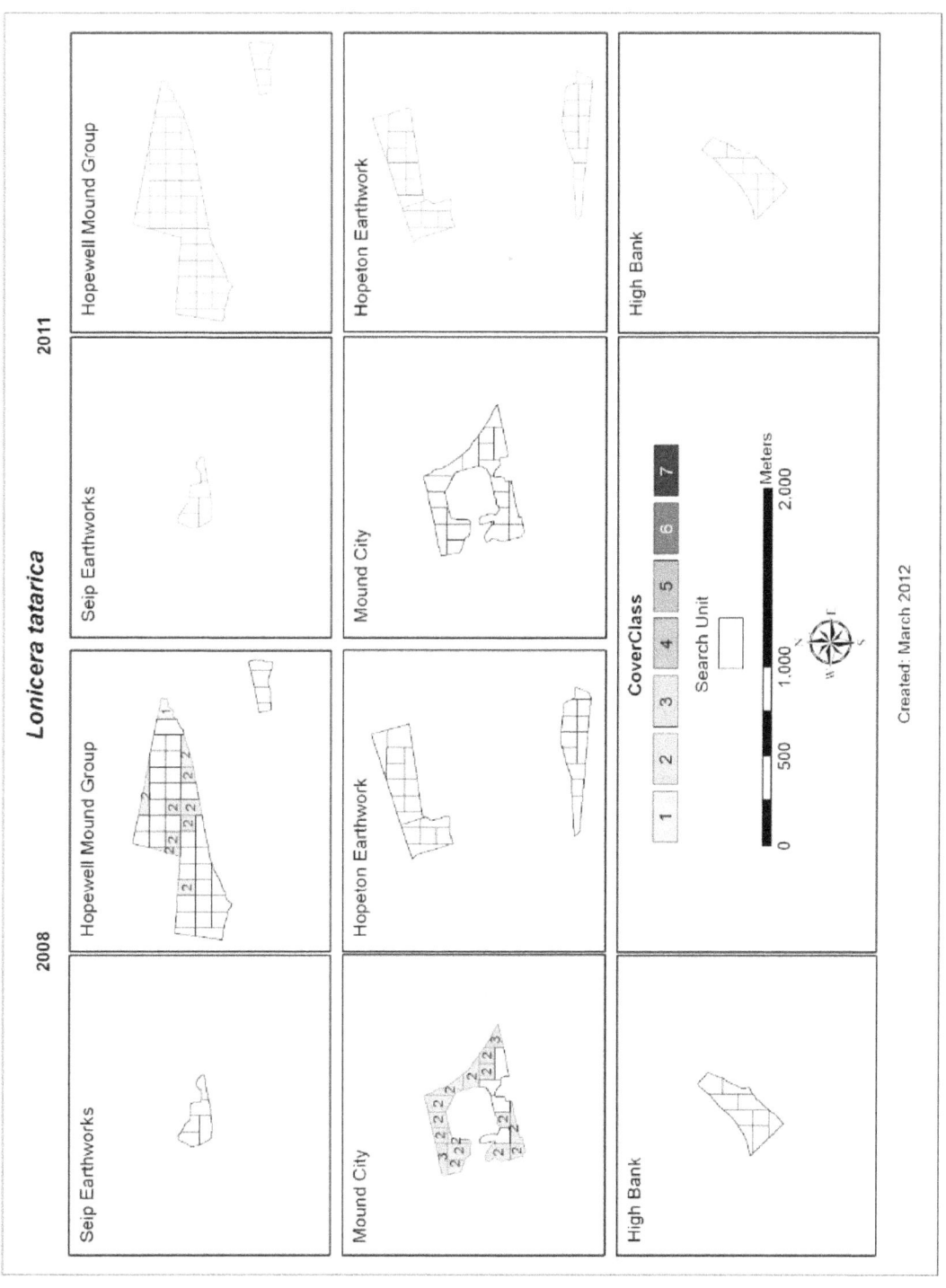

Figure 25. Abundance and distribution of *Lonicera tatarica* (Tatarian honeysuckle) at Hopewell Culture National Historical Park, 2008 and 2011. Cover classes are as follows: 1=0.1-0.9 m^2, 2=1-9.9 m^2, 3=10-49.9 m^2, 4= 50-99.9 m^2, 5=100-499.9 m^2, 6= 500-999.9 m^2, 7= 1,000-4,999 m^2.

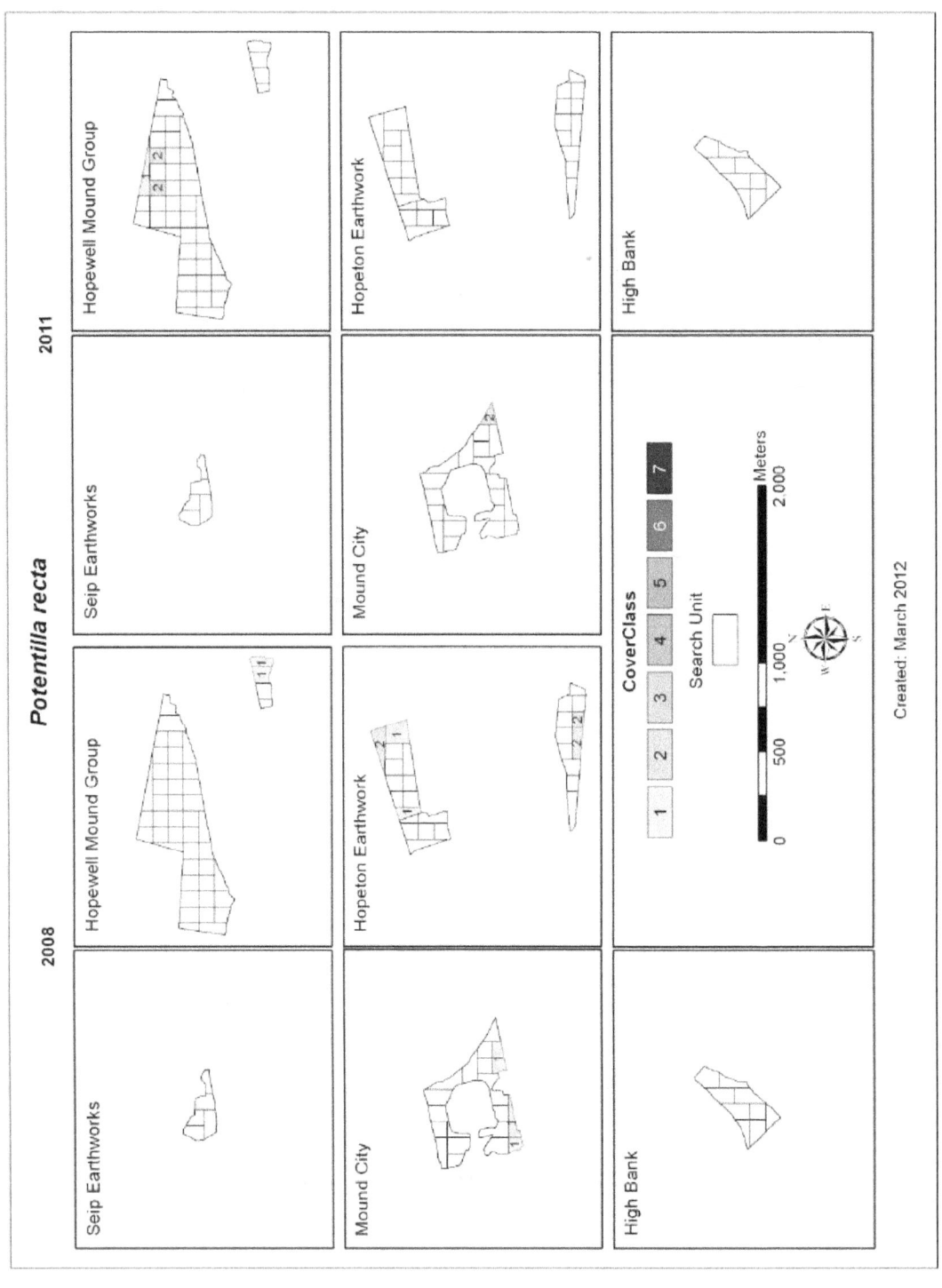

Figure 26. Abundance and distribution of *Potentilla recta* (sulphur cinquefoil) at Hopewell Culture National Historical Park, 2008 and 2011. Cover classes are as follows: 1=0.1-0.9 m^2, 2=1-9.9 m^2, 3=10-49.9 m^2, 4= 50-99.9 m^2, 5=100-499.9 m^2, 6= 500-999.9 m^2, 7= 1,000-4,999 m^2.

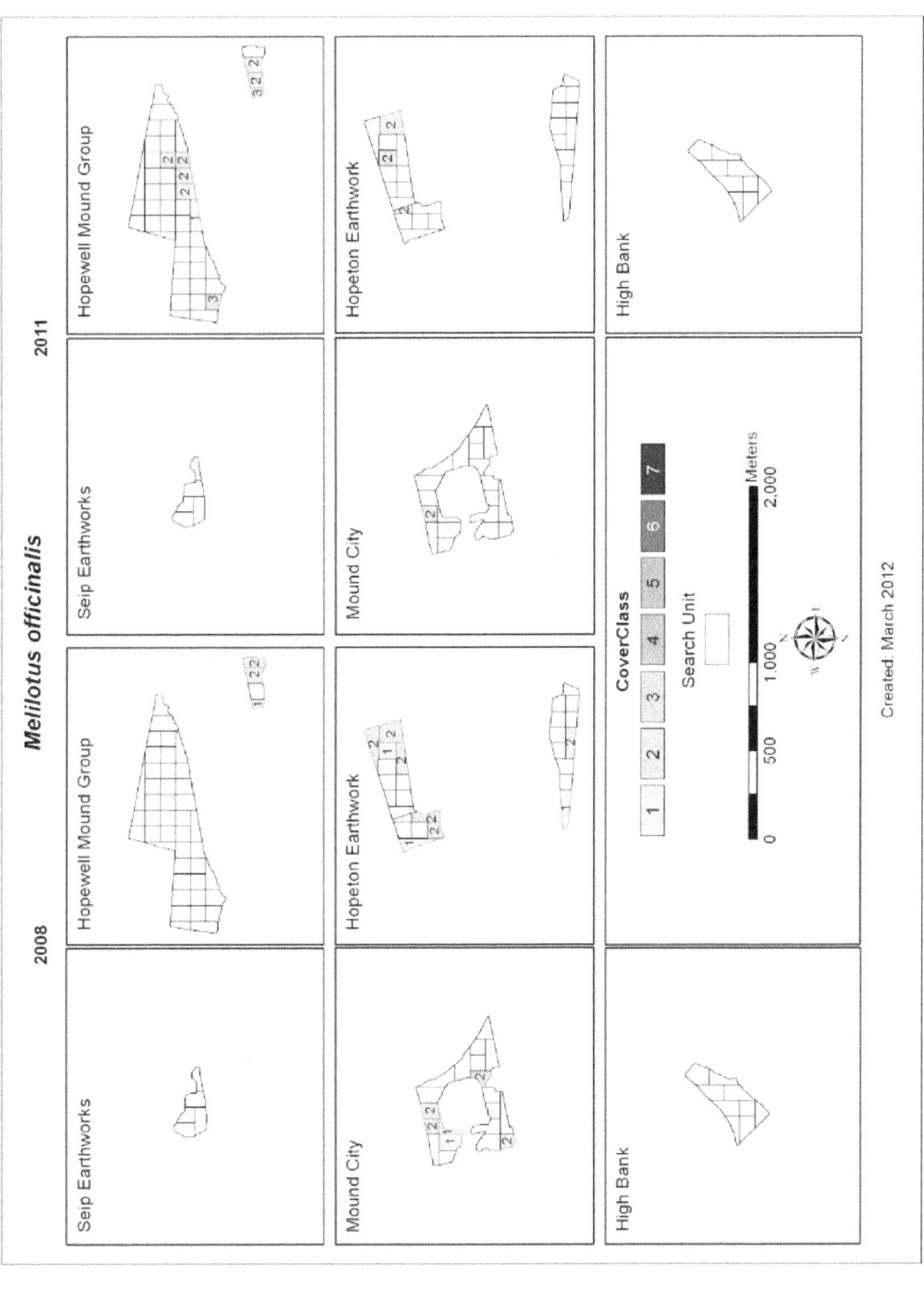

Figure 27. Abundance and distribution of *Melilotus officinalis* (sweetclover) at Hopewell Culture National Historical Park, 2008 and 2011. Cover classes are as follows: 1=0.1-0.9 m², 2=1-9.9 m², 3=10-49.9 m², 4= 50-99.9 m², 5=100-499.9 m², 6= 500-999.9 m², 7= 1,000-4,999 m².

37

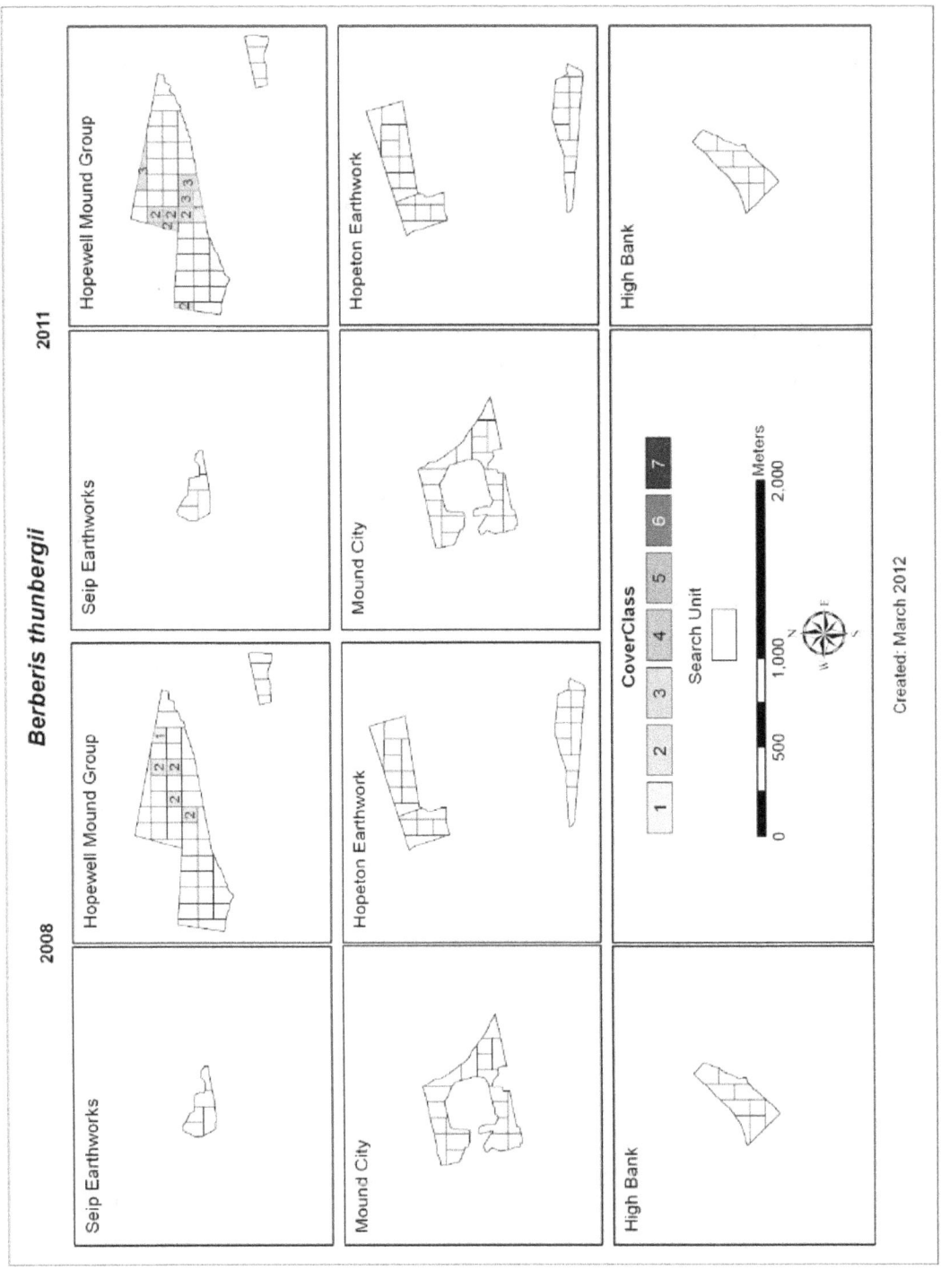

Figure 28. Abundance and distribution of *Berberis thunbergii* (Japanese barberry) at Hopewell Culture National Historical Park, 2008 and 2011. Cover classes are as follows: 1=0.1-0.9 m², 2=1-9.9 m², 3=10-49.9 m², 4= 50-99.9 m², 5=100-499.9 m², 6= 500-999.9 m², 7= 1,000-4,999 m².

38

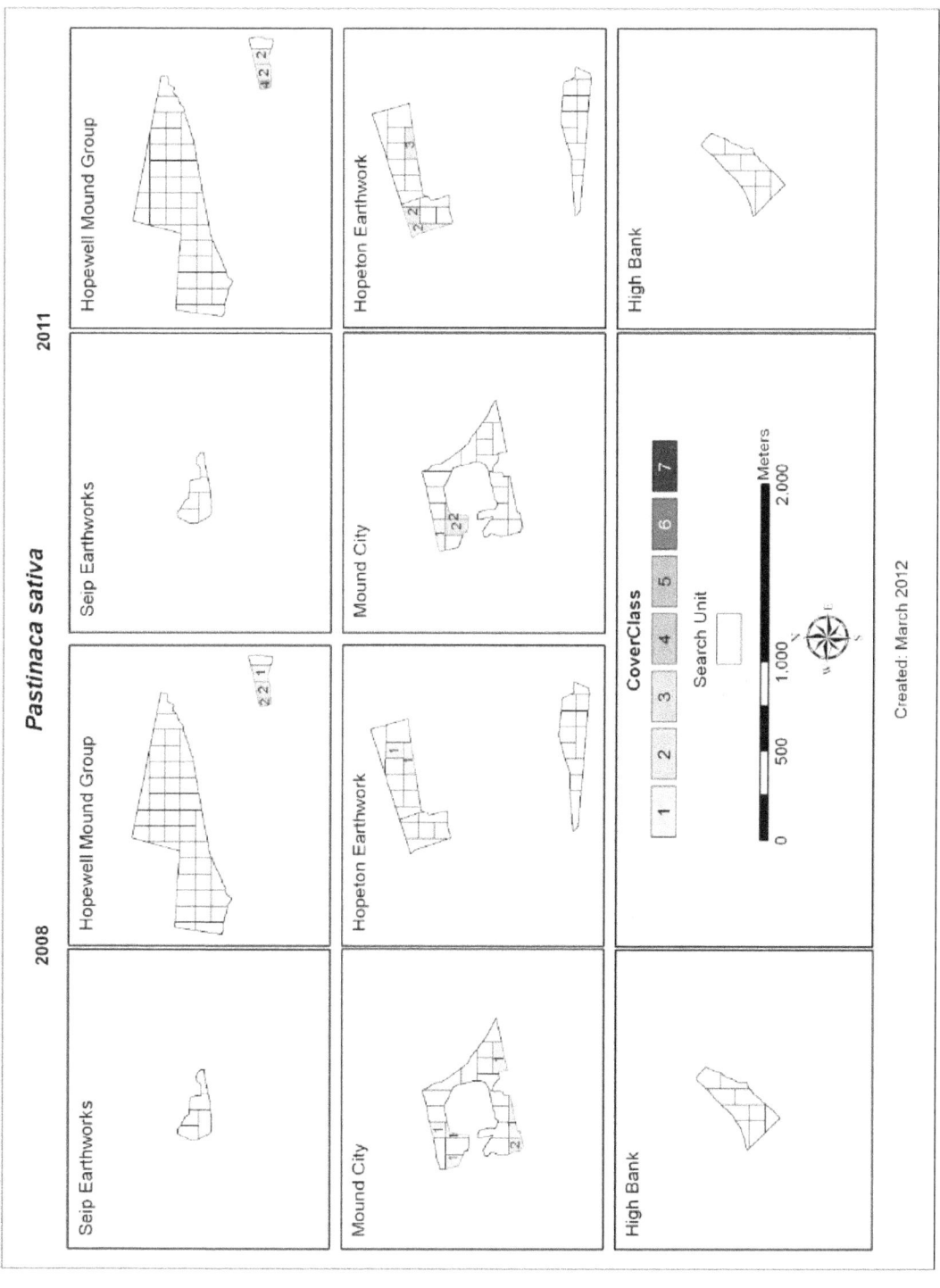

Figure 29. Abundance and distribution of *Pastinaca sativa* (common parsnip) at Hopewell Culture National Historical Park, 2008 and 2011. Cover classes are as follows: 1=0.1-0.9 m^2, 2=1-9.9 m^2, 3=10-49.9 m^2, 4= 50-99.9 m^2, 5=100-499.9 m^2, 6= 500-999.9 m^2, 7= 1,000-4,999 m^2.

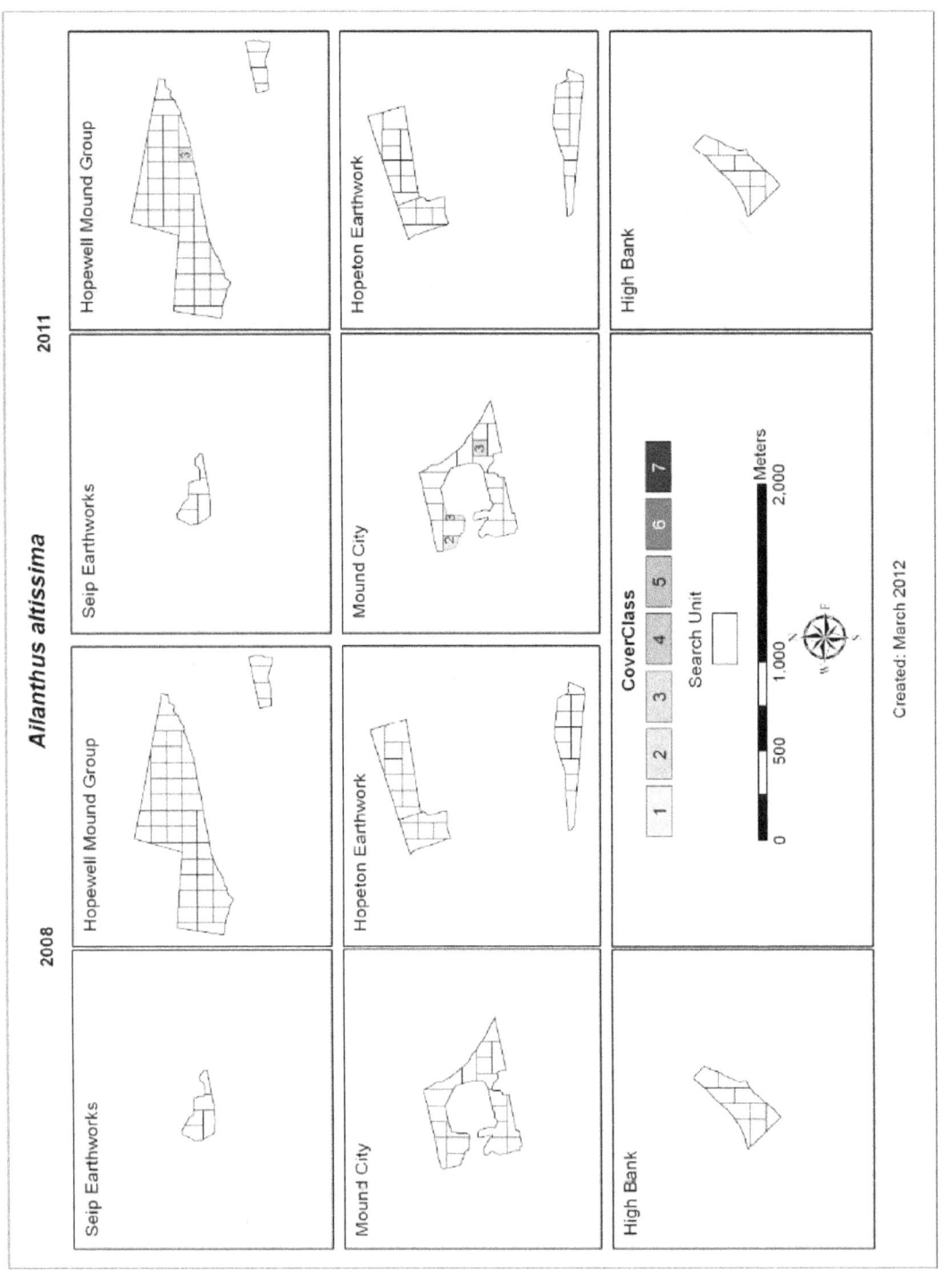

Figure 30. Abundance and distribution of *Ailanthus altissima* (tree-of-heaven) at Hopewell Culture National Historical Park, 2008 and 2011. Cover classes are as follows: 1=0.1-0.9 m², 2=1-9.9 m², 3=10-49.9 m², 4= 50-99.9 m², 5=100-499.9 m², 6= 500-999.9 m², 7= 1,000-4,999 m².

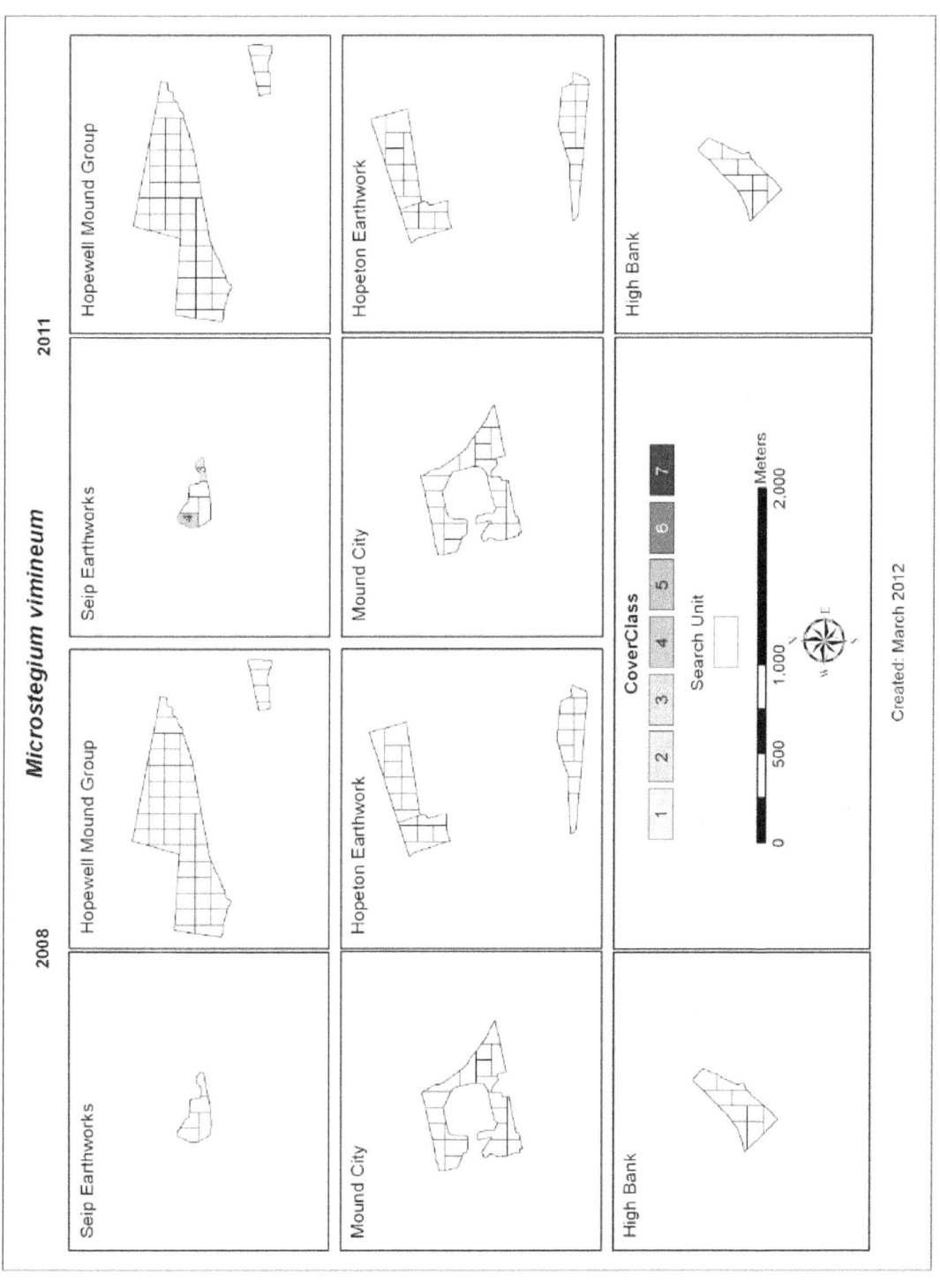

Figure 31. Abundance and distribution of *Microstegium vimineum* (Nepalese browntop) at Hopewell Culture National Historical Park, 2008 and 2011. Cover classes are as follows: 1=0.1-0.9 m^2, 2=1-9.9 m^2, 3=10-49.9 m^2, 4= 50-99.9 m^2, 5=100-499.9 m^2, 6= 500-999.9 m^2, 7= 1,000-4,999 m^2.

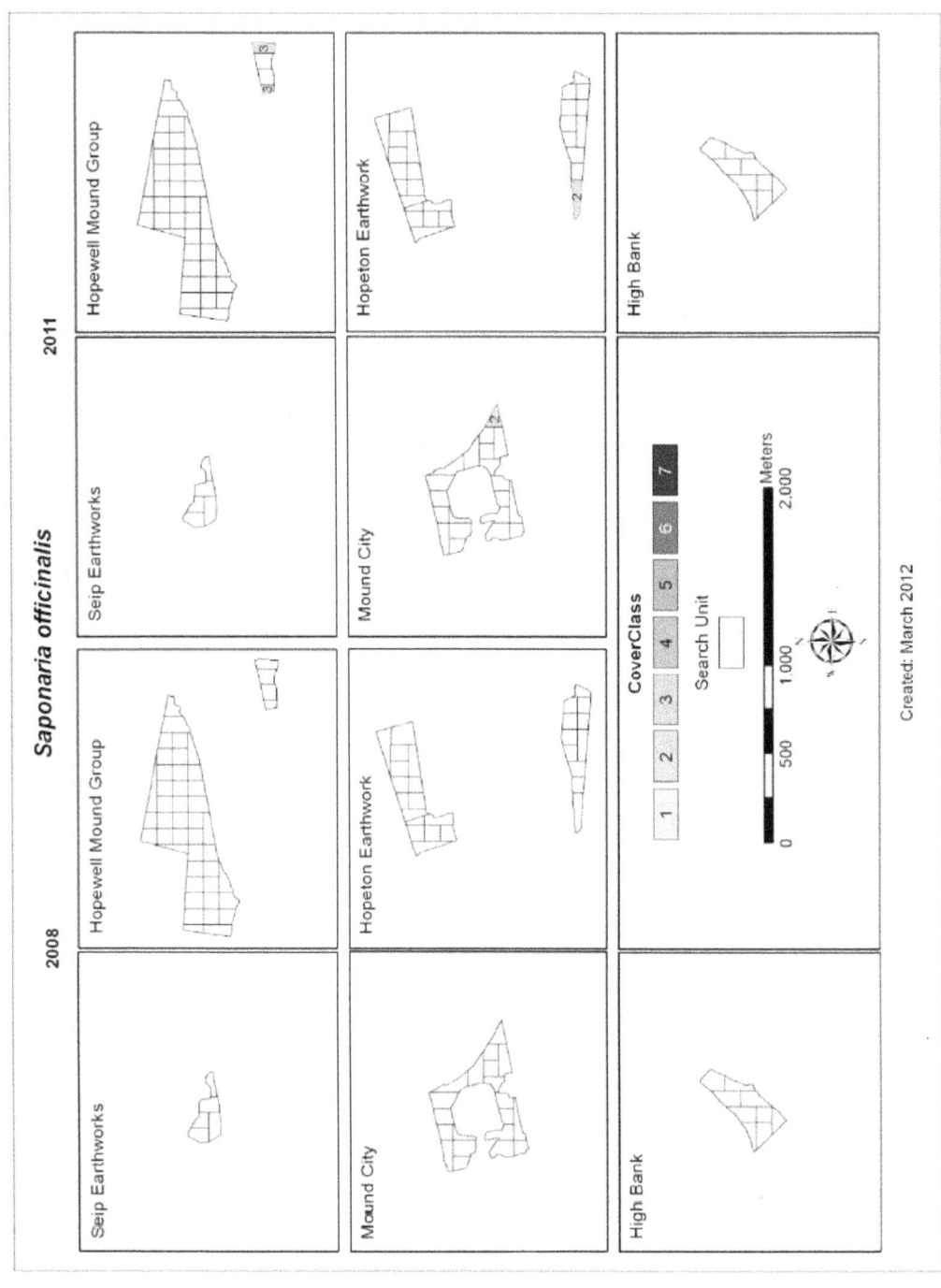

Figure 32. Abundance and distribution of *Saponaria officinalis* (bouncingbet) at Hopewell Culture National Historical Park, 2008 and 2011. Cover classes are as follows: 1=0. 1-0.9 m², 2=1-9.9 m², 3=10-49.9 m², 4= 50-99.9 m², 5=100-499.9 m², 6= 500-999.9 m², 7= 1,000-4,999 m².

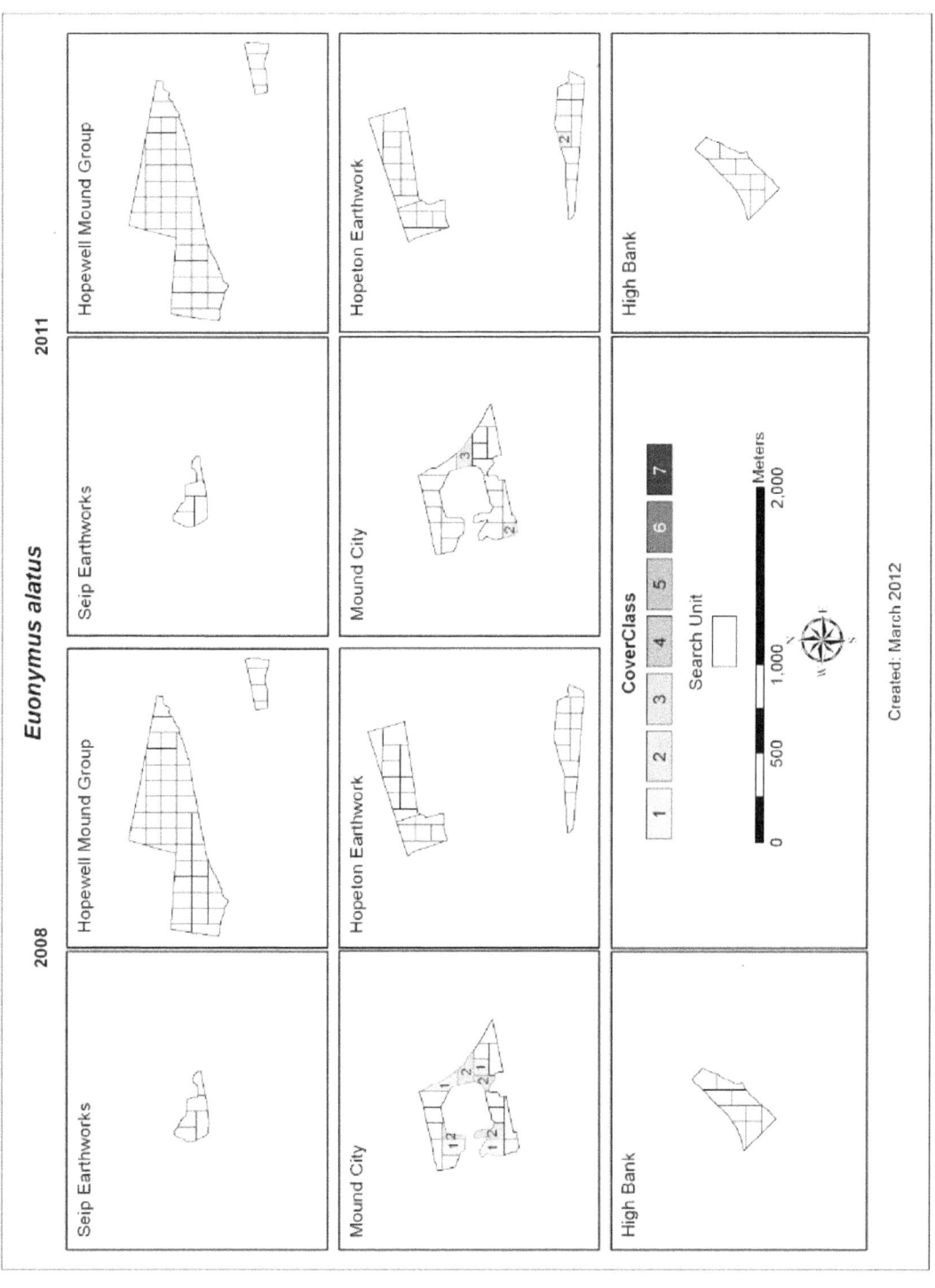

Figure 33. Abundance and distribution of *Euonymus alatus* (winged burningbush) at Hopewell Culture National Historical Park, 2008 and 2011. Cover classes are as follows: 1=0.1-0.9 m², 2=1-9.9 m², 3=10-49.9 m², 4= 50-99.9 m², 5=100-499.9 m², 6= 500-999.9 m², 7= 1,000-4,999 m².

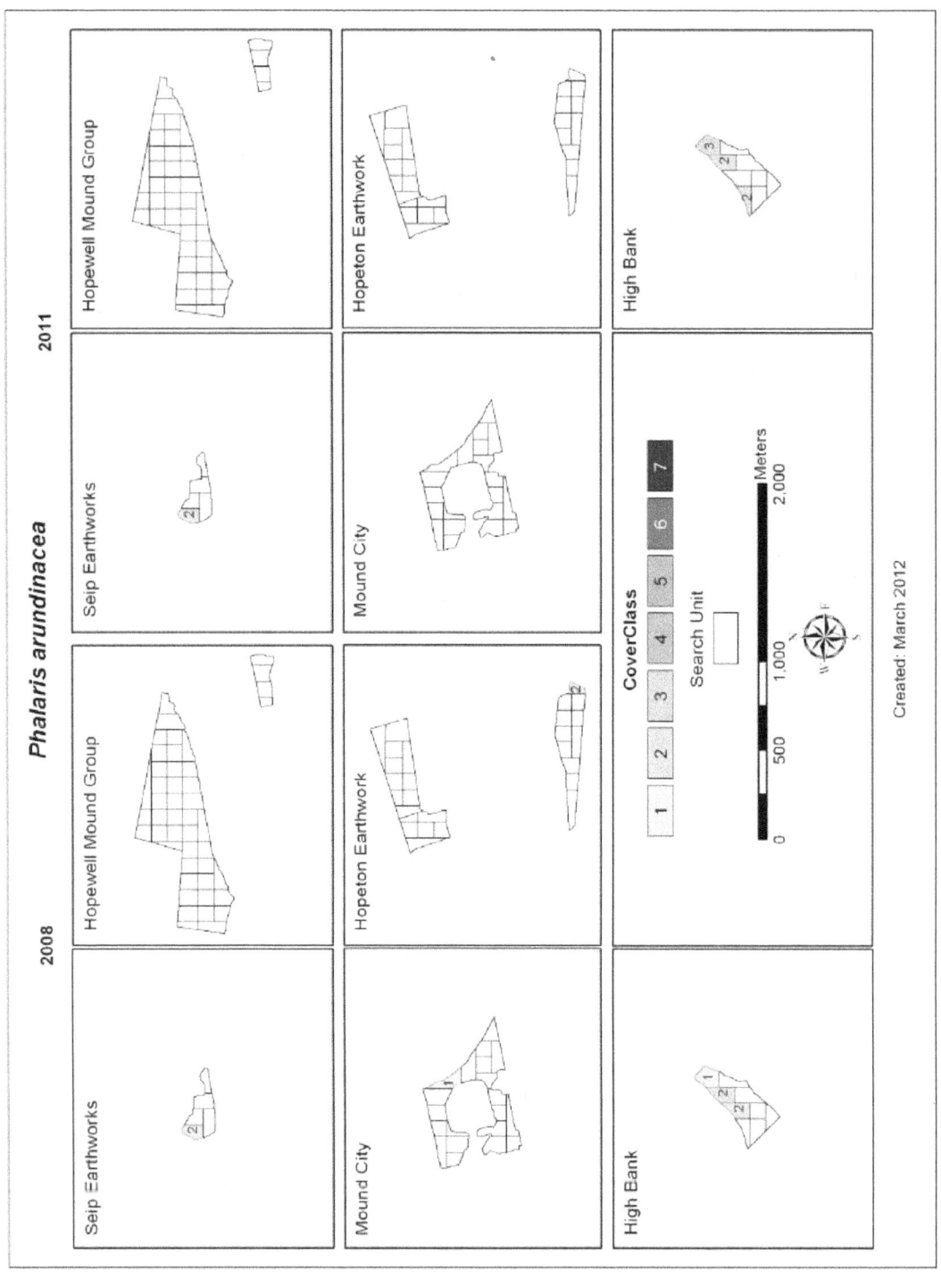

Figure 34. Abundance and distribution of *Phalaris arundinacea* (reed canarygrass) at Hopewell Culture National Historical Park, 2008 and 2011. Cover classes are as follows: 1=0.1-0.9 m^2, 2=1-9.9 m^2, 3=10-49.9 m^2, 4= 50-99.9 m^2, 5=100-499.9 m^2, 6= 500-999.9 m^2, 7= 1,000-4,999 m^2.

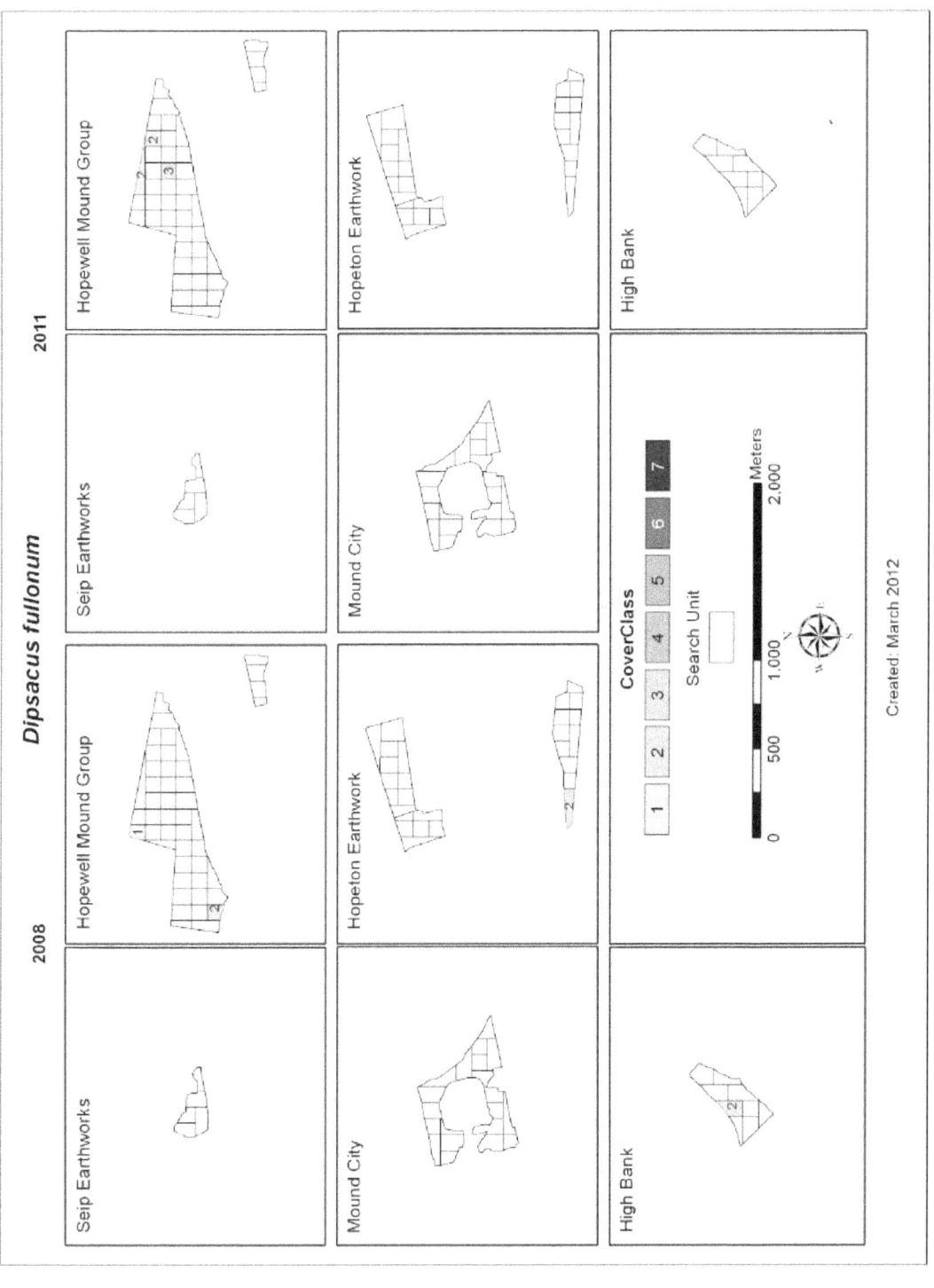

Figure 35. Abundance and distribution of *Dipsacus fullonum* (Fuller's teasel) at Hopewell Culture National Historical Park, 2008 and 2011. Cover classes are as follows: 1=0.1-0.9 m², 2=1-9.9 m², 3=10-49.9 m², 4= 50-99.9 m², 5=100-499.9 m², 6= 500-999.9 m², 7= 1,000-4,999 m².

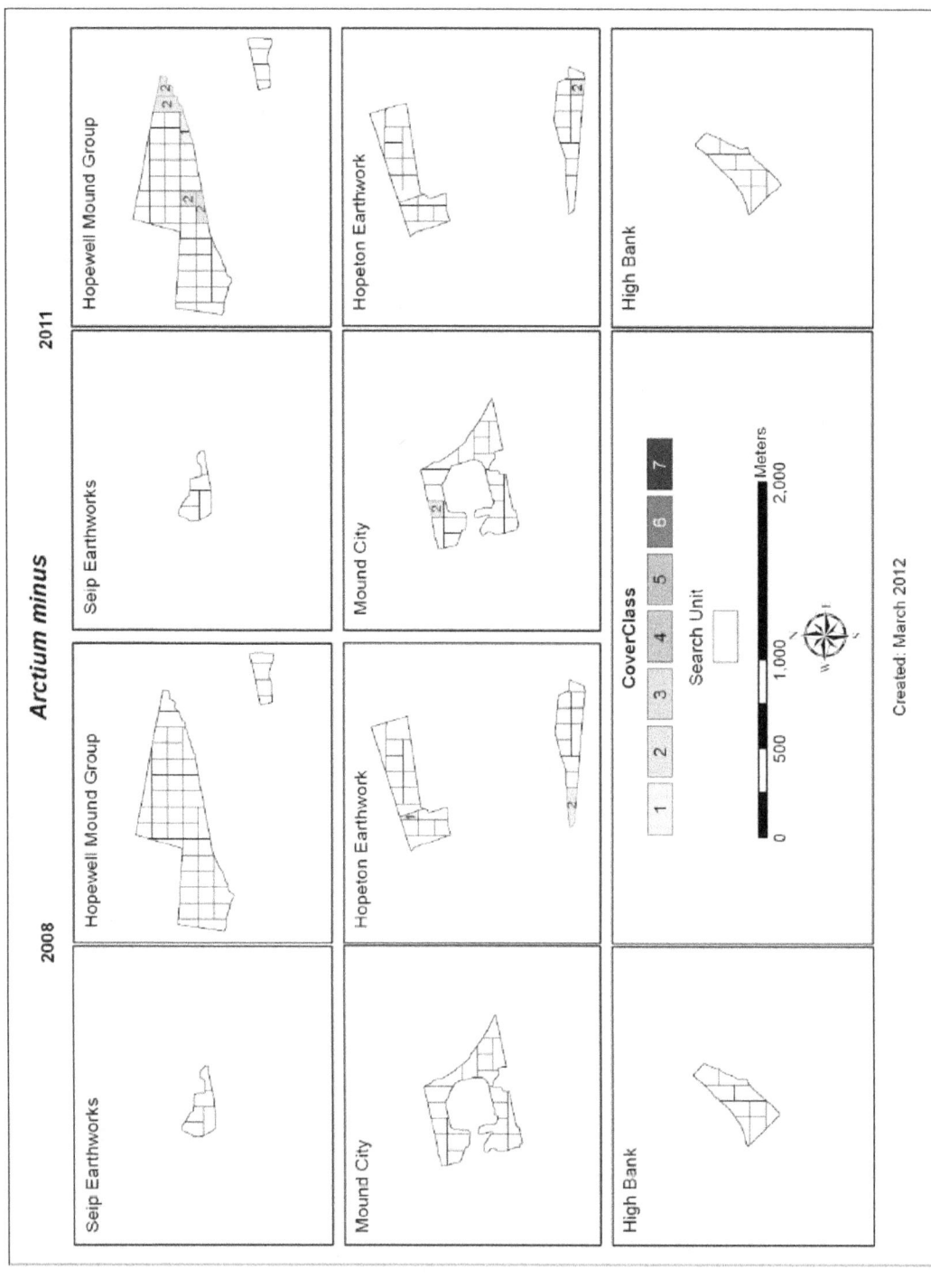

Figure 36. Abundance and distribution of *Arctium minus* (lesser burdock) at Hopewell Culture National Historical Park, 2008 and 2011. Cover classes are as follows: 1=0.1-0.9 m^2, 2=1-9.9 m^2, 3=10-49.9 m^2, 4= 50-99.9 m^2, 5=100-499.9 m^2, 6= 500-999.9 m^2, 7= 1,000-4,999 m^2.

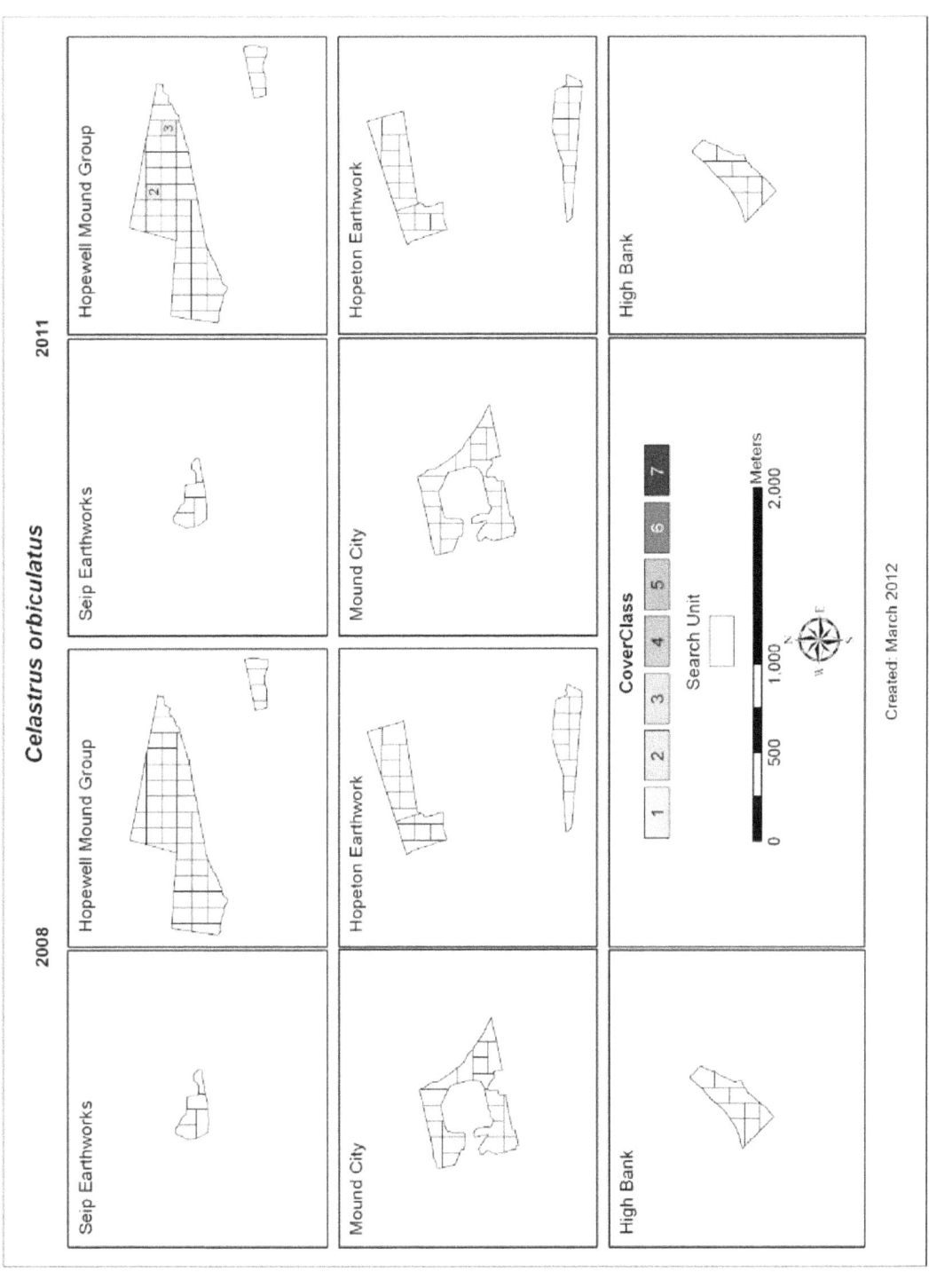

Figure 37. Abundance and distribution of *Celastrus orbiculatus* (Oriental bittersweet) at Hopewell Culture National Historical Park, 2008 and 2011. Cover classes are as follows: 1=0.1-0.9 m^2, 2=1-9.9 m^2, 3=10-49.9 m^2, 4= 50-99.9 m^2, 5=100-499.9 m^2, 6= 500-999.9 m^2, 7= 1,000-4,999 m^2.

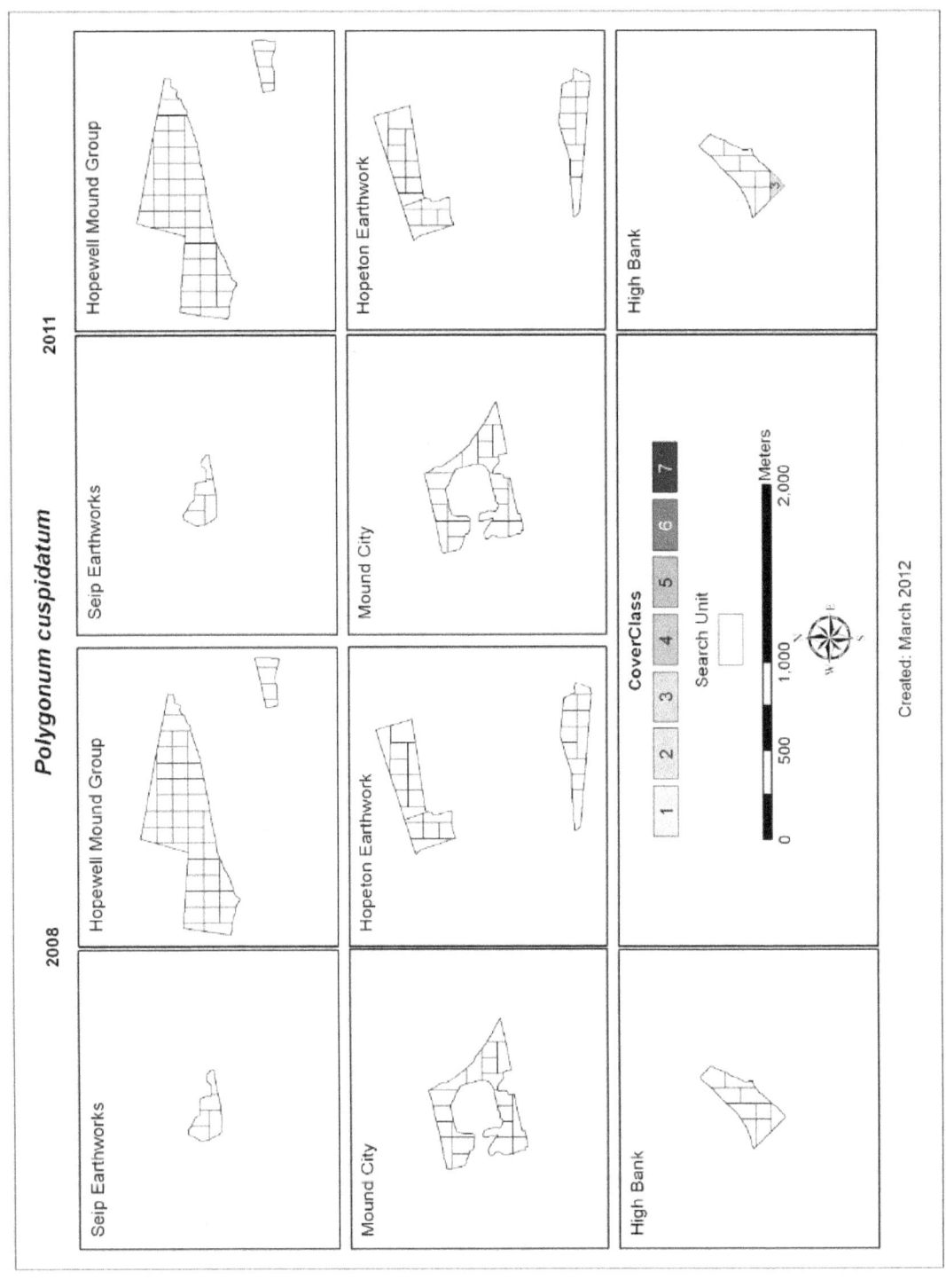

Figure 38. Abundance and distribution of *Polygonum cuspidatum* (Japanese knotweed) at Hopewell Culture National Historical Park, 2008 and 2011. Cover classes are as follows: 1=0.1-0.9 m², 2=1-9.9 m², 3=10-49.9 m², 4= 50-99.9 m², 5=100-499.9 m², 6= 500-999.9 m², 7= 1,000-4,999 m².

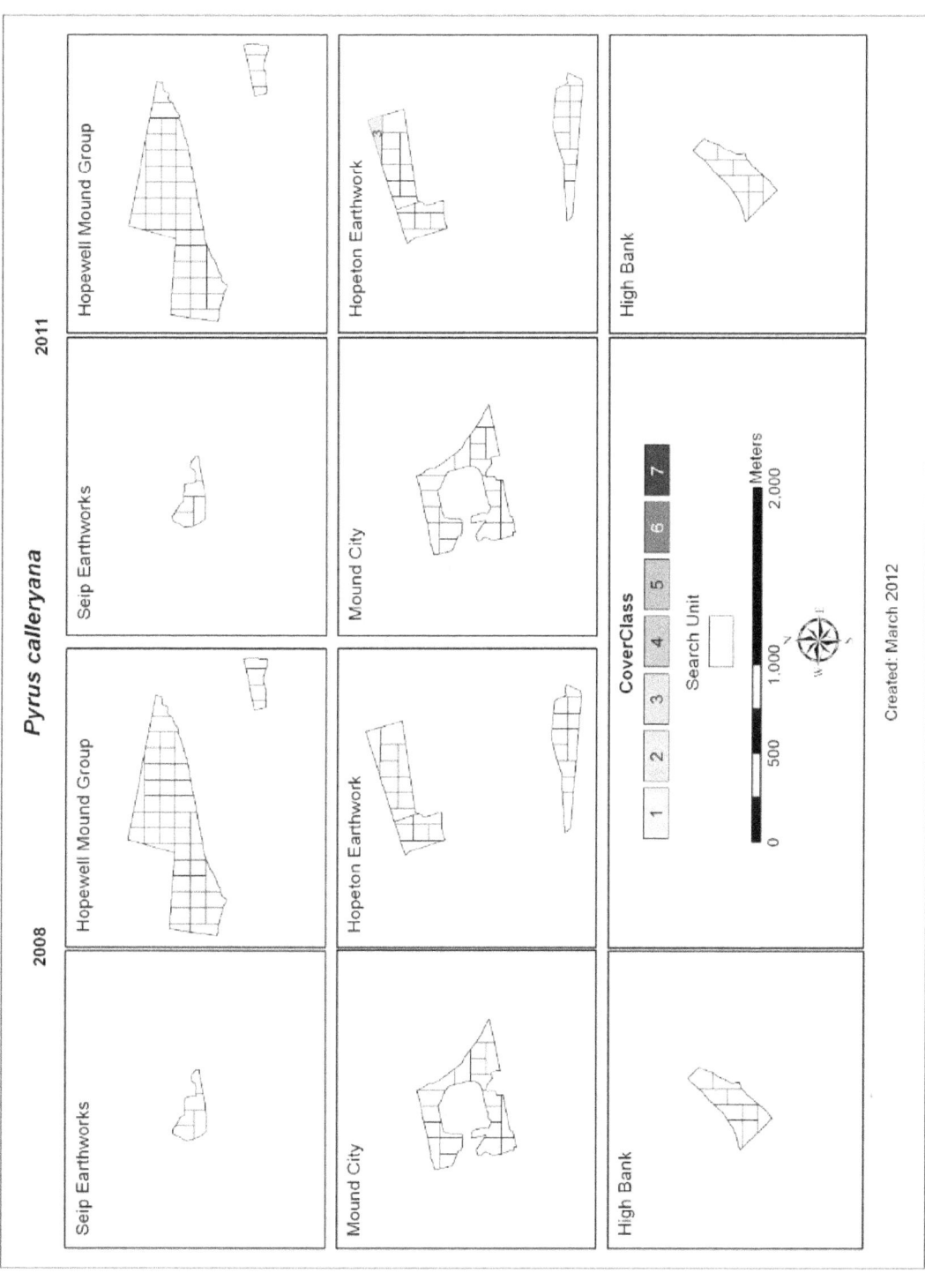

Figure 39. Abundance and distribution of *Pyrus calleryana* (Callery pear) at Hopewell Culture National Historical Park, 2008 and 2011. Cover classes are as follows: 1=0.1-0.9 m^2, 2=1-9.9 m^2, 3=10-49.9 m^2, 4= 50-99.9 m^2, 5=100-499.9 m^2, 6= 500-999.9 m^2, 7= 1,000-4,999 m^2.

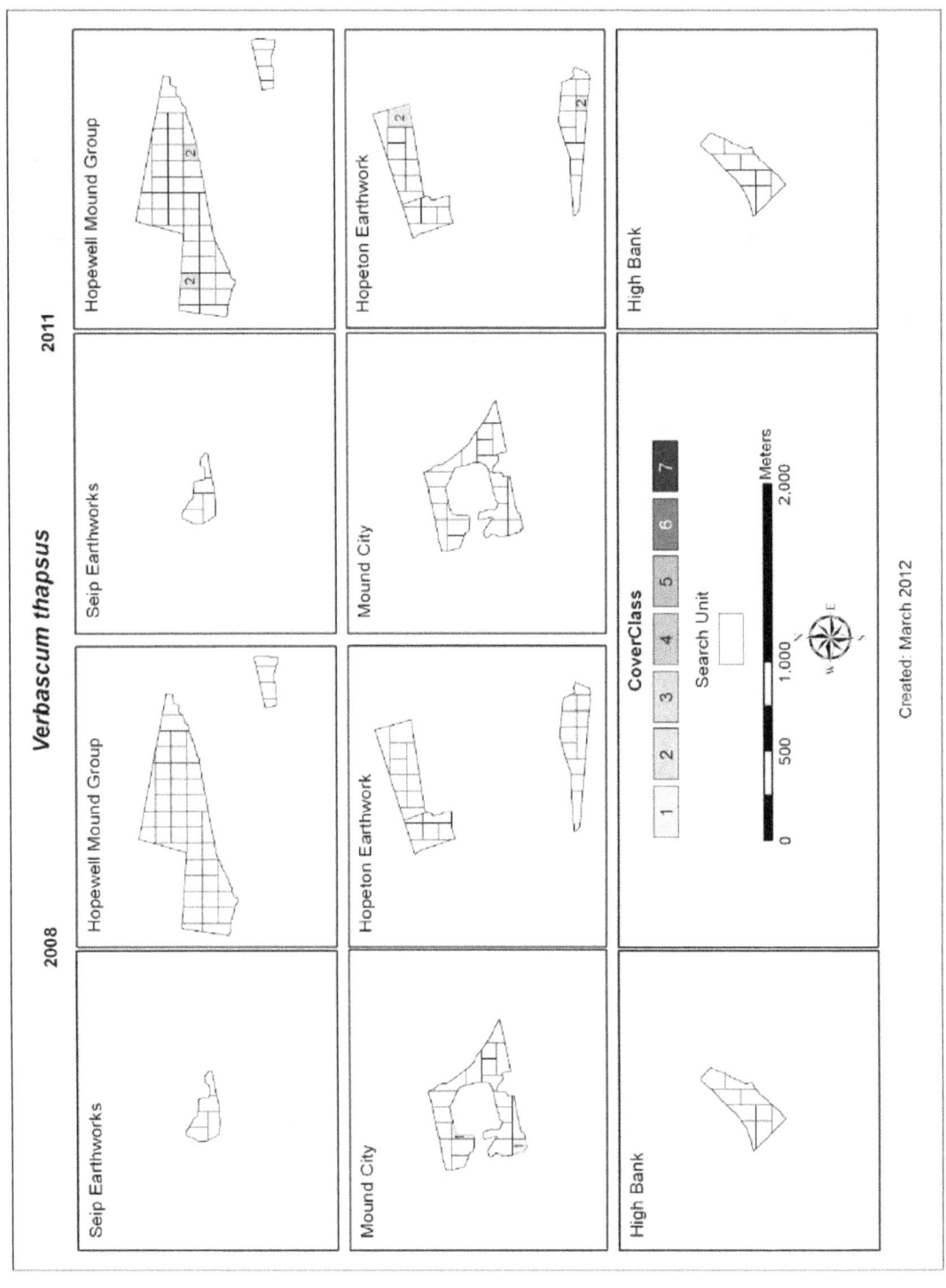

Figure 40. Abundance and distribution of *Verbascum thapsus* (common mullein) at Hopewell Culture National Historical Park, 2008 and 2011. Cover classes are as follows: 1=0.1-0.9 m², 2=1-9.9 m², 3=10-49.9 m², 4= 50-99.9 m², 5=100-499.9 m², 6= 500-999.9 m², 7= 1,000-4,999 m².

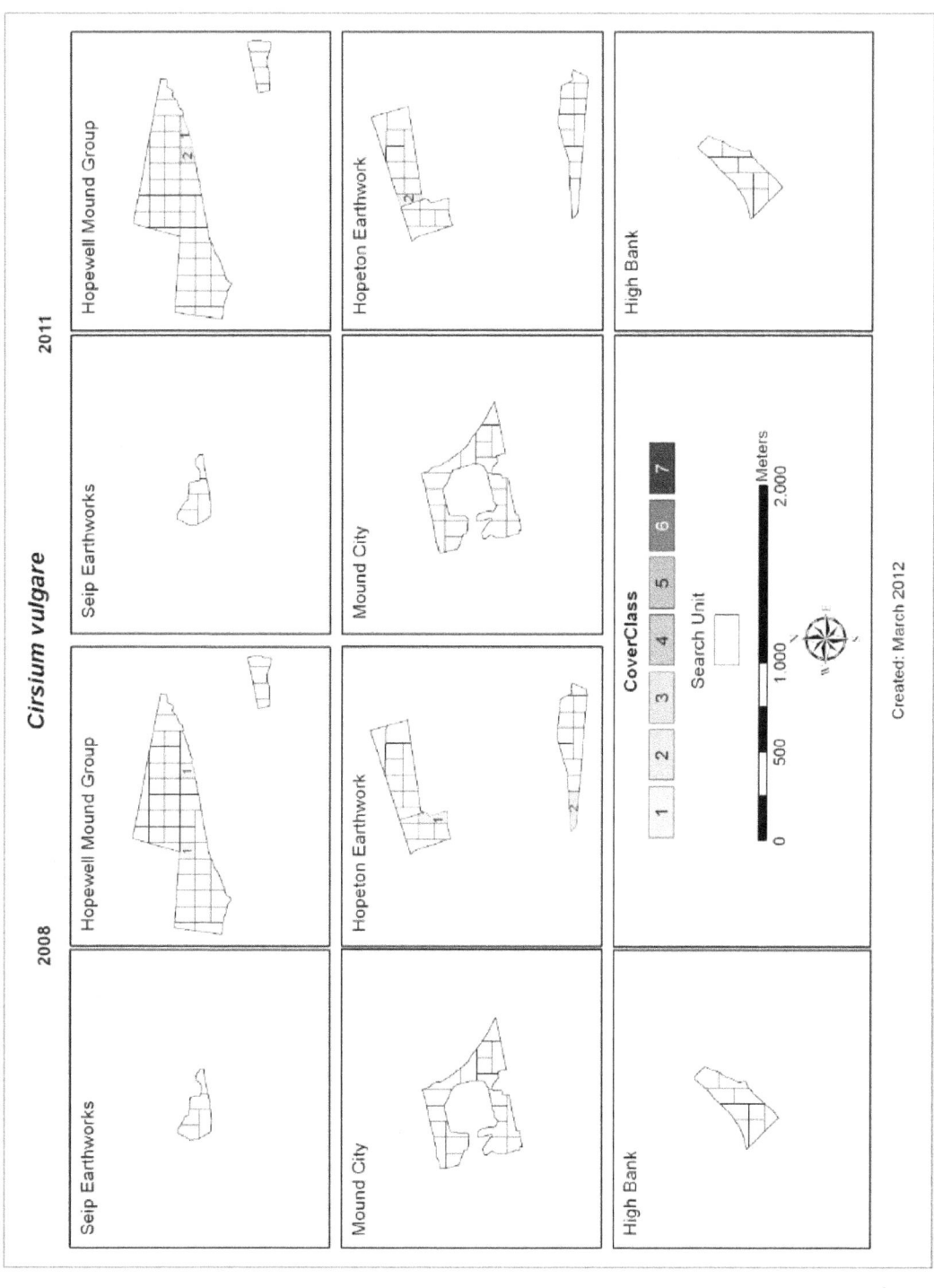

Figure 41. Abundance and distribution of *Cirsium vulgare* (bull thistle) at Hopewell Culture National Historical Park, 2008 and 2011. Cover classes are as follows: 1=0.1-0.9 m², 2=1-9.9 m², 3=10-49.9 m², 4= 50-99.9 m², 5=100-499.9 m², 6= 500-999.9 m², 7= 1,000-4,999 m².

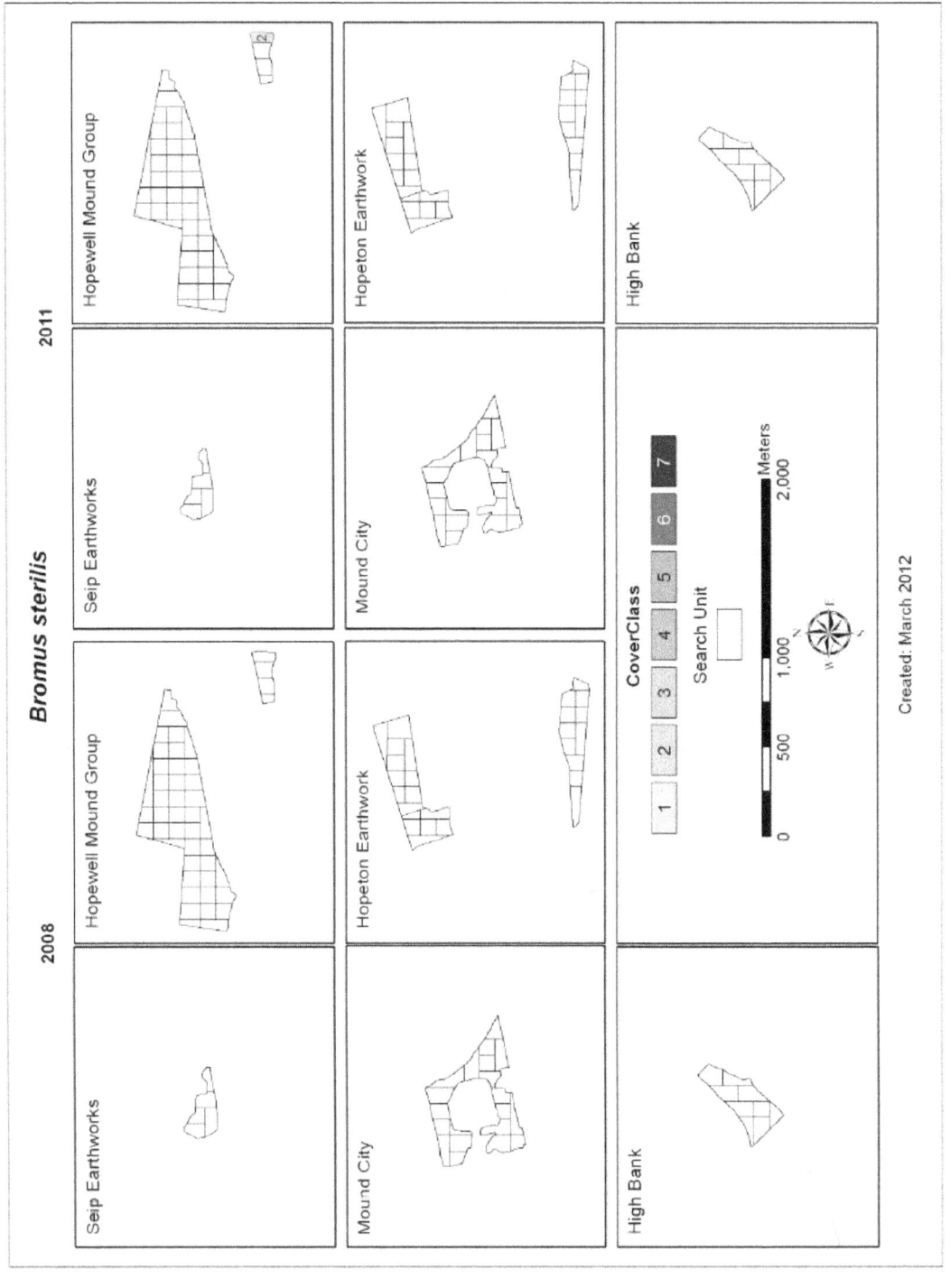

Figure 42. Abundance and distribution of *Bromus sterilis* (poverty brome) at Hopewell Culture National Historical Park, 2008 and 2011. Cover classes are as follows: $1= 0.1-0.9$ m^2, $2= 1-9.9$ m^2, $3= 10-49.9$ m^2, $4= 50-99.9$ m^2, $5= 100-499.9$ m^2, $6= 500-999.9$ m^2, $7= 1,000-4,999$ m^2.

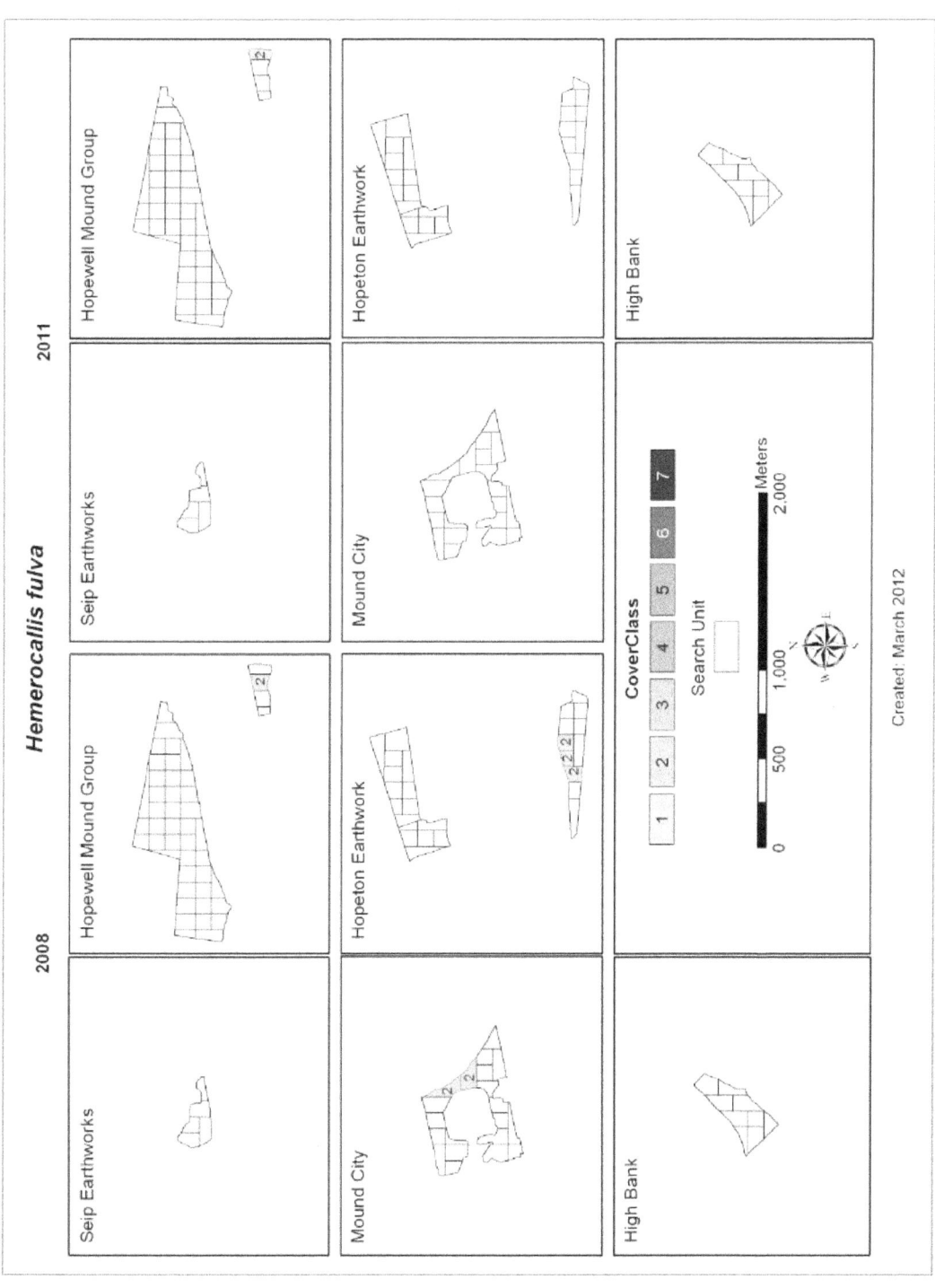

Figure 43. Abundance and distribution of *Hemerocallis fulva* (orange daylilly) at Hopewell Culture National Historical Park, 2008 and 2011. Cover classes are as follows: 1=0.1-0.9 m², 2=1-9.9 m², 3=10-49.9 m², 4= 50-99.9 m², 5=100-499.9 m², 6= 500-999.9 m², 7= 1,000-4,999 m².

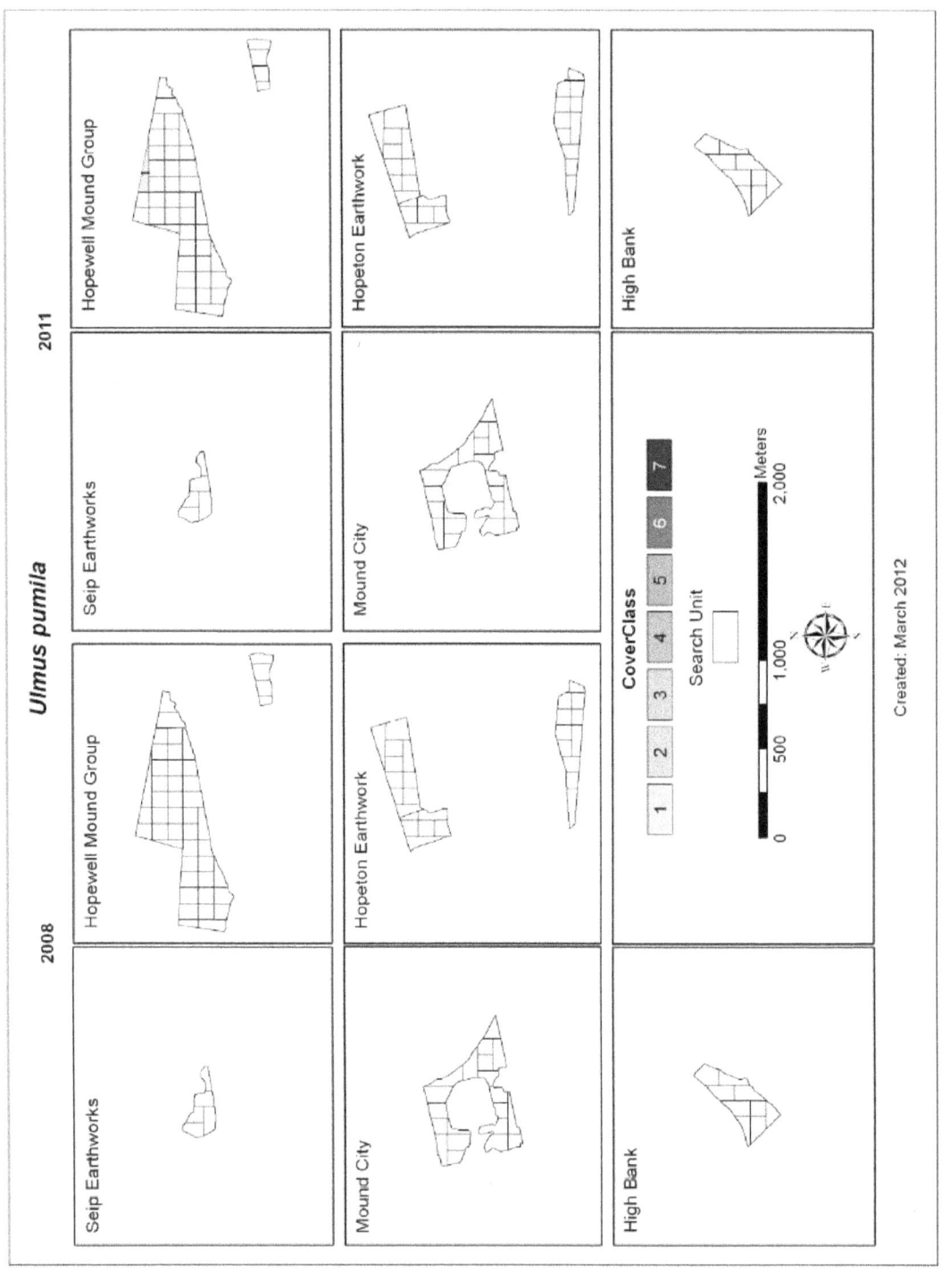

Figure 44. Abundance and distribution of *Ulmus pumila* (Siberian elm) at Hopewell Culture National Historical Park, 2008 and 2011. Cover classes are as follows: 1=0.1-0.9 m², 2=1-9.9 m², 3=10-49.9 m², 4= 50-99.9 m², 5=100-499.9 m², 6= 500-999.9 m², 7= 1,000-4,999 m².

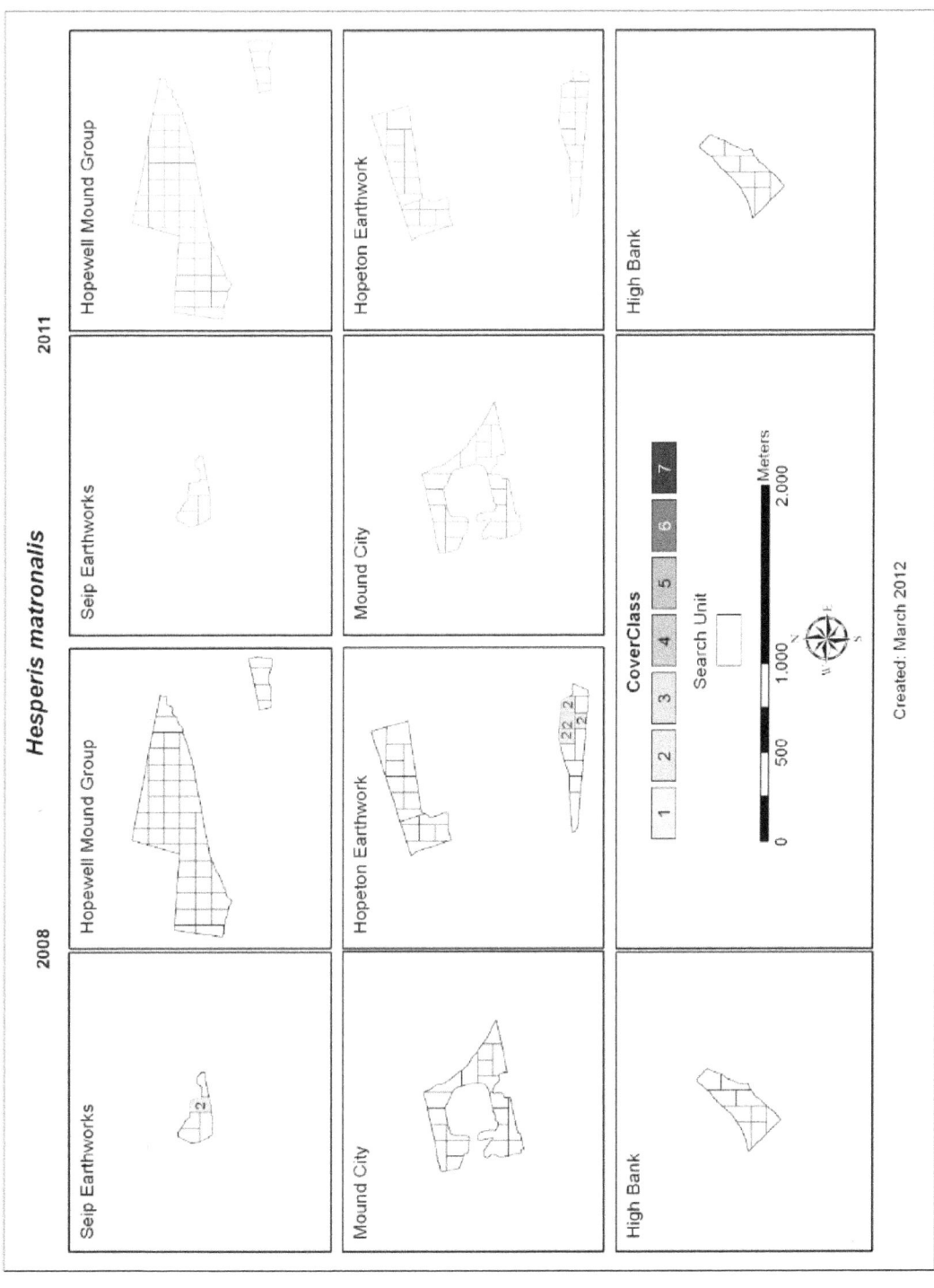

Figure 45. Abundance and distribution of *Hesperis matronalis* (dame's rocket) at Hopewell Culture National Historical Park, 2008 and 2011. Cover classes are as follows: $1=0.1-0.9 \text{ m}^2$, $2=1-9.9 \text{ m}^2$, $3=10-49.9 \text{ m}^2$, $4=50-99.9 \text{ m}^2$, $5=100-499.9 \text{ m}^2$, $6=500-999.9 \text{ m}^2$, $7=1,000-4,999 \text{ m}^2$.

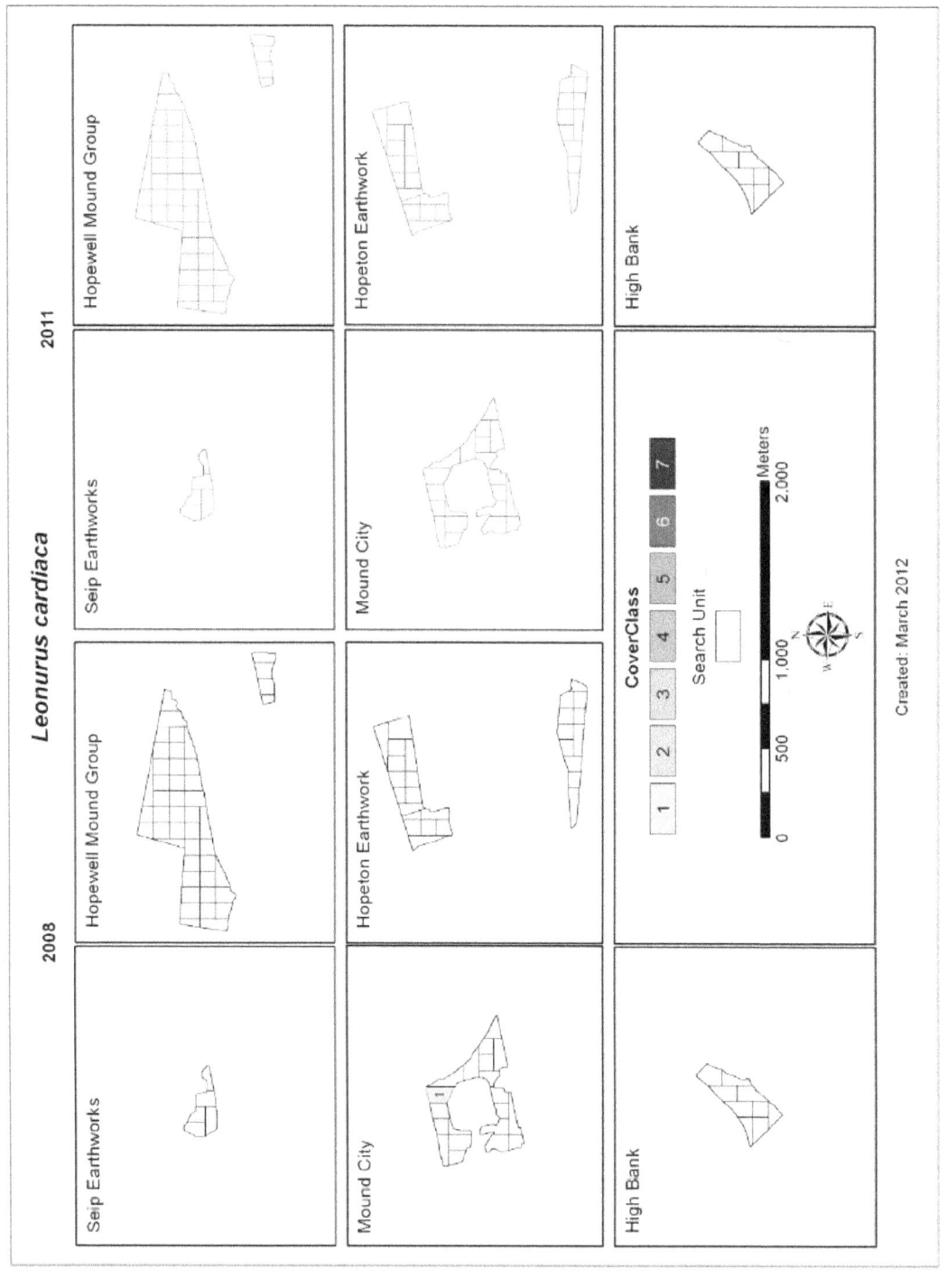

Figure 46. Abundance and distribution of *Leonurus cardiaca* (common motherwort) at Hopewell Culture National Historical Park, 2008 and 2011. Cover classes are as follows: 1=0.1-0.9 m^2, 2=1-9.9 m^2, 3=10-49.9 m^2, 4= 50-99.9 m^2, 5=100-499.9 m^2, 6= 500-999.9 m^2, 7= 1,000-4,999 m^2.

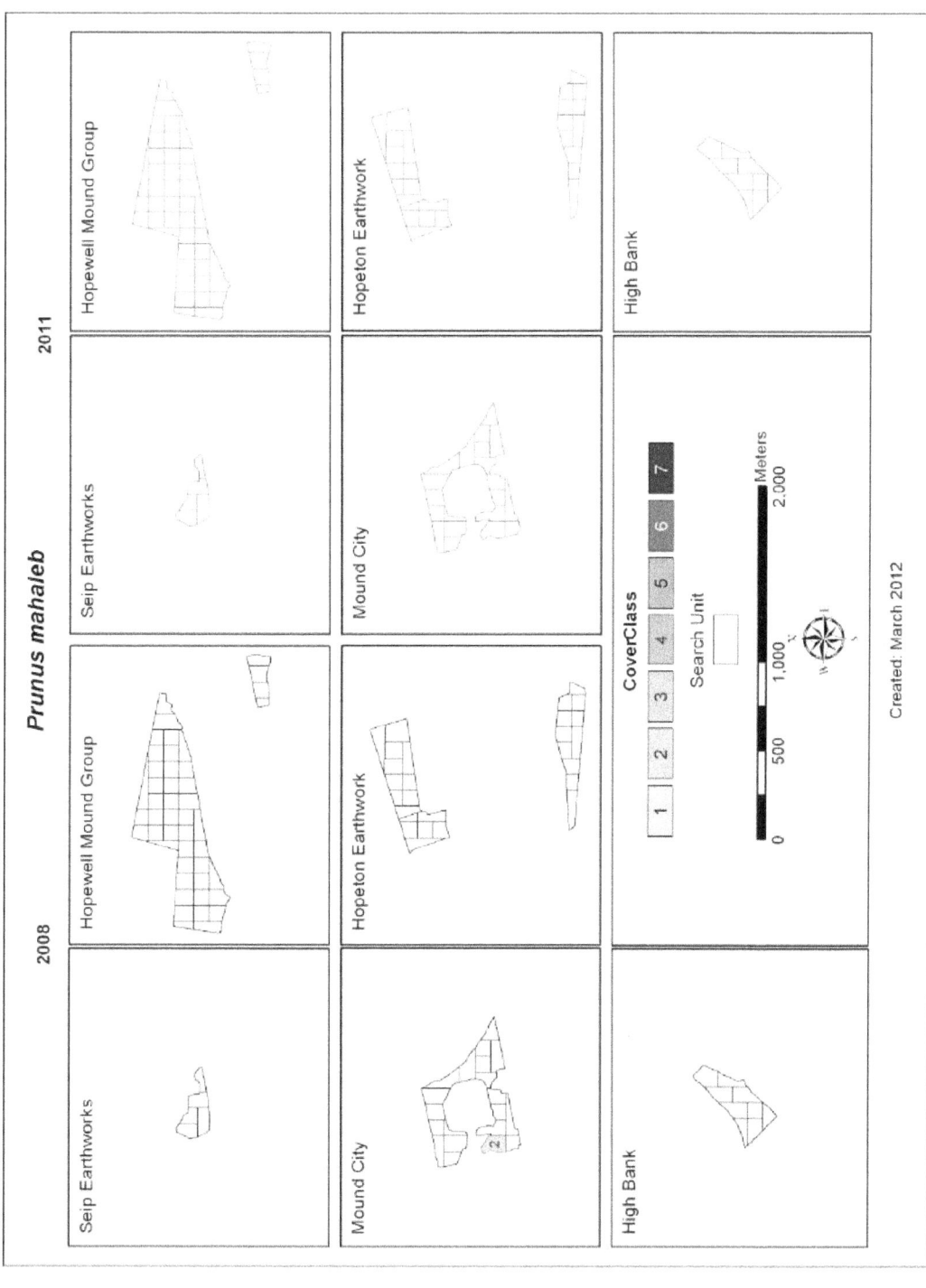

Figure 47. Abundance and distribution of *Prunus mahaleb* (Mahaleb's cherry) at Hopewell Culture National Historical Park, 2008 and 2011. Cover classes are as follows: 1=0.1-0.9 m², 2=1-9.9 m², 3=10-49.9 m², 4= 50-99.9 m², 5=100-499.9 m², 6= 500-999.9 m², 7= 1,000-4,999 m².